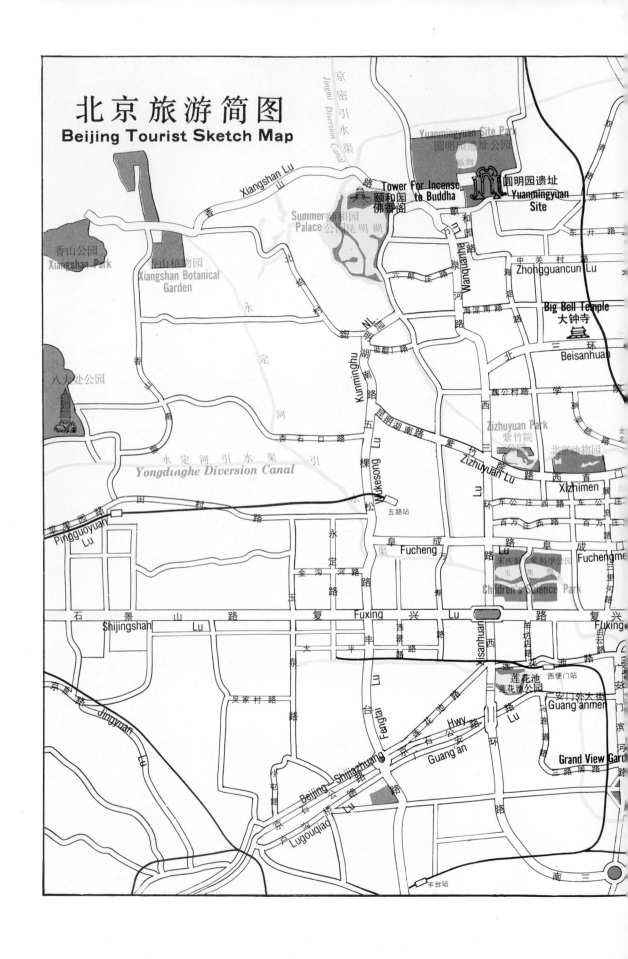

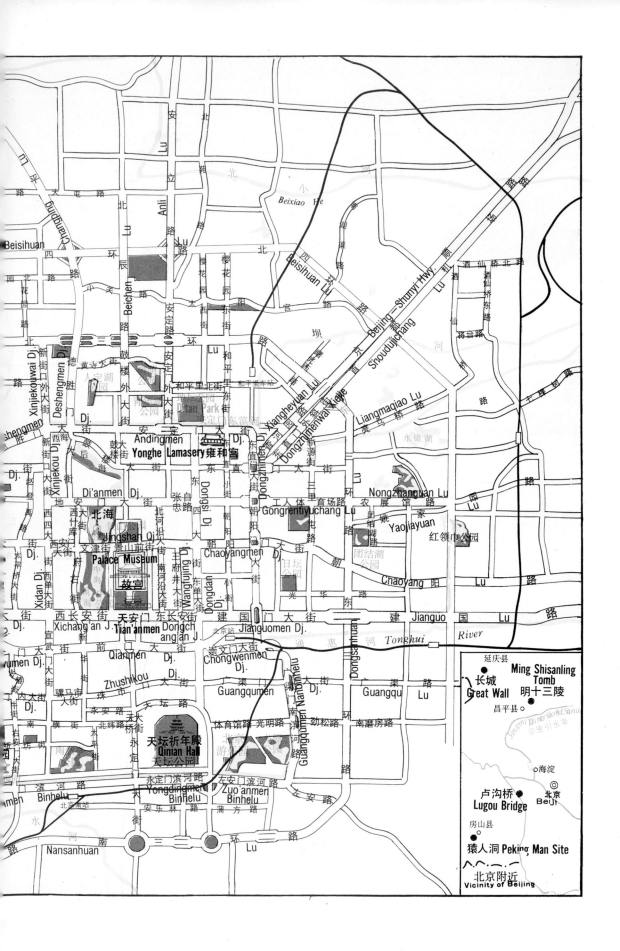

北京名胜

Best Sights in Beijing

北京名胜

BEST SIGHTS IN BEIJING

China Esperanto Press, Beijing, China

ISBN 7-5052-0157-3

Published by the China Esperanto Press, P.O. Box 77, Beijing, China

Distributed by China International Book Trading Corporation
35 Chegongzhuang Xilu, Beijing 100044, China
P.O. Box 399, Beijing, China

Printed in the People's Republic of China

目 录

Contents

前　言

北京是中华人民共和国的首都,世界历史文化名城。

自 70 万年前"北京猿人"在这里繁衍、生息以来,历经旧石器时代和新石器时代,这里一直是中华民族文化的摇篮,也是人类文明的发祥地之一。

作为城池,北京兴建于商代(约前 16 世纪——约前 11 世纪)后期,那时这里有燕和蓟两个自然形成的方国。公元前 1045 年,周(约前 11 世纪——前 256 年)灭商,分封诸侯,周武王封帝尧之后于蓟,封召公奭于燕,北京始为方国之都。三千年来,尽管朝代屡屡更迭,城名也多次更换,但北京一直是中国北方的军事重镇和贸易中心,在其发展过程中,由偏居一隅的封国都城,跃居为几代名声赫赫的帝都。

北京地处华北平原北端,西、北、东三面环山,东南为平原。地理学家把这块平原形象地称为"北京湾"。古人曾以"北枕居庸,西峙太行,东连山海,南俯中原"来说明北京地理位置的重要。

公元 10 世纪上半叶,崛起于中国东北方的少数民族契丹族兵强马壮,越过拱卫在北京湾三面的莽莽群山,举兵南下,进入华北北部,攻占了蓟城,并把它定为辽(公元 907 - 1125 年)的陪都,因为蓟位于它所辖区域的南部,所以改称南京,又称燕京。一个多世纪以后,中国东北方的另一个少数民族女真族起兵灭辽,建立了金(公元 1115 - 1234 年),并于 1153 年迁都燕京,改称中都。女真族在燕京整整统治了 100 年,后因受到新兴蒙古族的进攻,被迫迁都汴京(今河南开封),随后蒙古族铁骑入占中都。1267 年蒙古族首领忽必烈下令在中都东北郊筑建新城,4 年后这位首领即在兴建中的都城内登上皇帝宝座。又过了 15 年,新城全部建成,这就是意大利旅行家马可·波罗在他游记中称之为"世界莫能与比"的元大都。从此,北京取代了长安、洛阳、汴梁等古都的地位,成为中国的政治、经济、军事、文化中心,并延至明(公元 1368 - 1644 年)、清(公元 1616－1911 年)两代。

公元 1368 年，曾经是和尚的朱元璋借助农民起义军的力量，推翻了元(1206－1368 年)帝国，建立了明王朝，以应天(今江苏南京)为京师。朱元璋做了 30 年皇帝，死后，其孙朱允炆继位，史称建文帝。可惜好景不长，他的叔父燕王朱棣在自己的封地北平府起兵，发动"靖难之役"，经过三年的酷烈战争，于 1402 年攻入应天，夺取了帝位，翌年改元永乐，并诏"以北平为北京"，决定迁都北京。从此，全国各地的能工巧匠云集北京，开始营建城垣、宫殿、坛庙和苑囿，工程浩大，其规模远远超过了元大都。至 1421 年，主要工程基本完工，朱棣正式迁都北京。

明代的北京城参照应天即南京城的规制而建，分宫城、皇城、内城和外城四重，整座城池方方正正。城的四周建有高大坚固的砖墙，四面对称地洞开 16 个拱形门，门洞上的城楼飞檐凌空。立于城楼，可以远眺数十里。在城的中央，至今仍保存完好的紫禁城是它的心脏。紫禁城的周围是整齐如畦、经纬分明的街巷，两旁排列着商铺、民居。弯曲的河流，美丽的苑囿，庄严神幻的古代祭坛和寺庙，戒备森严、建筑豪华的署衙官宅，错落其间，方直中融入环曲，对称中显现变化。这座具有恢宏气势和浓郁的东方色彩的古城，标志着中国的古代文明又进入到一个新的辉煌时期。

明朝的统治延续了 270 多年。1644 年李自成领导的农民军打进北京城，皇帝朱由检走投无路，吊死在紫禁城后的煤山。同年，清世祖爱新觉罗·福临进关，入主北京，建立了清王朝。同历代王朝一样，新朝皇帝总是要对他居住的京城大兴土木。由于民族岐视的缘故，清代实行旗、民分城居住的制度。八旗官兵及其家属圈占内城民宅，原来的居民一律搬至外城居住，北京城因此不得不增建官邸，扩充民房。清顺治 2 年(1645 年)，皇室重建紫禁城的太和、中和、保和三大殿。顺治 8 年重修承天门，竣工后，改称天安门。其间，还开发和拓展了"三海"（南海、中海、北海）皇家园林。到了18世纪中叶，清代兴修园林之风大盛，仅在京城西北郊扩建和新建的大型园林就有5座。与此同时，信佛奉道流行，修庙造塔、建寺筑观成为普遍现象。据《乾隆京城全图》标绘，北京城有胡同1400余条，寺庙竟有1300余座。那时的北京城馆阁连绵，殿宇栉比，牌匾相望；市面店铺林立，商贾云集。清代国势达到极盛，成为亚洲最强大的国家。

但是，到了近代即1840年以后，清朝国势日衰，特别是在1860年第二次鸦片战争时期，英法联军攻入北京，许多宫殿和著名的"三山五园"被联军放火烧毁，无数珍宝被劫掠到异国他乡。如今要重睹旧时北京的全部风貌和这里曾经出现过的某些波澜壮阔的历史场景已不可能。然而，当人们置身于它的城区或郊野，面对那些触目皆是的历史遗迹，却会使你感到过去的事物仿佛又回到了眼前。一座巍峨耸立的古塔，常常凝聚着一代匠人的艺术精华；一块风蚀斑驳的碑石，或许记载着一件轰动一时的壮举；一片荒草丛生、瓦砾狼藉的宫苑废址，往往引发人们无限的忧思。当人们走进紫禁城太和殿的时候，不能不联想到皇帝的金冠龙袍和奢靡无度；当人们登上万里长城的时候，眼前似乎浮现出"烽火连天远，铁骑鏖战急"的厮杀场景；当人们在颐和园昆明湖荡舟的时候，面对湖光山色，会情不自禁地体味到"若道湖光宛似镜，阿谁不是镜中人"的佳境……北京是一座宏大的历史博物馆，走进去，就感到它的历史悠久；北京是一座巨大的游乐园，走进去，就会乐而忘返。

北京，作为几代王朝的都城和中华人民共和国的首都，其古迹胜景不胜枚举，我们从中精选13佳景编辑成《北京名胜》，以飨读者。本画册是北京悠久历史和美丽风姿的缩影，也可作为来京观光者的导游手册。愿它给朋友们带来方便和愉快。

Foreword

Beijing, capital of the People's Republic of China, is a famous historical and cultural city. It is a cradle of Chinese civilization and one of the birthplaces of mankind. As early as 700,000 years ago Peking Man began to inhabit the region and lived through the Old and New Stone Ages.

Two dukedoms, Yan and Ji, were established and built the city of Ji during the late Shang Dynasty (c. 16th-11th century B.C.). The city was situated very close to the present city of Beijing. In 1045 B.C. the Zhou Dynasty (c. 11th century-256 B.C.) overthrew the Shang Dynasty and bestowed the land of Ji to a descendent of King Rao and the land of Yan to Shi, Duke of Zhao. The name of the city of Ji changed many times over 3,000 years, but it remained a strategic point and a trade center and kept growing in size. It was made national capital for several dynasties.

Beijing lies at the northern tip of the North China Plains. To its west, north and east are mountain ranges; to its southeast is flat land. Geographers call the Beijing area "Beijing Bay". An ancient book describes Beijing as such: "Its head rests on the Juyong Pass; the Taihang Mountains rise to its west; to its east are mountains and the sea; and it overlooks a plain to its south."

In the early 10th century Qidan, a nomadic tribe in northeast China, grew strong, marched over the mountains into the north part of the North China Plains, took the city of Ji and made it secondary capital of the Liao Dynasty (907-1125). Because Ji was located in the southern part of their territory, the Qidan called it Nanjing, or South Capital, and also Yanjing. One century later, another tribe named Nuzhen overthrew the Liao Dynasty and established the Jin Dynasty (1115-1234). In 1153 they moved their capital to Yanjing and changed its name to Zhongdu. After another century, the Nuzhen were forced out of Zhongdu by the emerging power of Mongols and moved their capital to Pianjing (present-day Kaifeng in Henan Province). In 1267 Kublai Khan, chief of the Mongols, issued an order to build a new city to the northeast of the old city of Zhongdu. Kublai Khan ascended the throne in the new city four years later. But the new city was not totally completed in another 15 years. The new city was named Dadu, capital of the Yuan Dynasty, described by Marco Polo as a city "unmatchable in the world". Since then Beijing replaced Chang'an, Luoyang, Bianliang and other cities as the national capital and became the political, economic, military and cultural center of China through the Yuan (1206-1368), Ming (1368-1644) and Qing dynasties (1644-1911).

In 1368 Zhu Yuanzhang, once a poor Buddhist monk, led a peasant uprising to overthrow the Yuan Dynasty and founded the Ming Dynasty. He set his capital in Yingtian (present-day Nanjing in Jiangsu Province). He stayed on the throne for 30 years and was succeeded by his grandson Zhu Yunwen (Emperor Wen Di). Zhu Li, Duke of Yan, a son of Zhu Yuanzhang, launched a war to usurp the power from his nephew, the new emperor. After three years of bloody wars, his troops occupied Yingtian in 1402. Zhu Li became Emperor Yong Le and moved the national capital from Yingtian to his base in Beijing. He summoned craftsmen from all over the country to renovate the city wall and the imperial palace and build temples and gardens. The size of the city was greatly enlarged. By 1421 main projects had been completed and Zhu Li formally established his capital in Beijing.

The city of Beijing was a copy of the city of Nanjing. It was divided into four squares one inside another: the Imperial Palace, Imperial City, Inner City and Outer City. Sixteen gates in a symmetrical partern were located on the four sides of the Inner City. Standing on an imposing city gate tower one could see as far as several dozen kilometers away. The Imperial Palace, also known as Forbidden City, was located in the center of Beijing. Spreading from it in a neat pattern were streets flanked with stores and residential houses. Streams flew through lakes and gardens. Temples and official mansions had majestic buildings.

The Ming Dynasty lasted for 270 years. In 1644 Li Zicheng and his peasant rebels entered Beijing. Zhu Youjian, the last emperor of the Ming dynasty, hanged himself on a hill behind the Imperial Palace. In the same year, Aisin Gioro Fu Lin, the chief of the Manchus, came to Beijing from north of the Great Wall, chased away Li Zicheng, and founded the Qing Dynasty. As earlier emperors, he carried out a large scale renovation of the city. The troops of the Manchu Eight Banners were allowed to take any houses they liked in the Inner City. The original residents were forced to move to the Outer City. Many grand mansions were built to accommodate the new rulers. In 1645 the imperial court began to rebuild the Taihe, Zhonghe and Baohe halls in the Imperial Palace and in 1651 to rebuild the Chengtian Gate, which, upon completion, was renamed Tian'anmen, or the Gate of Heavenly Peace. During the same period, the Nanhai (South Sea), Zhonghai (Middle Sea) and Beihai (North Sea) lakes were dredged and enlarged to become imperial gardens. Construction of gardens reached its heyday in the middle of the 18th century. Five large-scale gardens were built or renovated in the northeastern suburbs. Taoism was developing fast during the Qing Dynasty. A great number of Taoist temples were built. A map of the capital made during Emperor Qian Long's Reign marks out 1,400 side streets in Beijing and 1,300 temples. At that time, grand towers and halls stood one after another; stores lined many streets. China became the strongest country in Asia during the 18th century.

But the Qing Dynasty declined rapidly after 1840. In 1860, during the second Opium War, British and French troops invaded Beijing and looted and burnt the imperial gardens and palaces. Numerous treasures were taken out of China.

The present Beijing offers many places of historical significance. The ancient pagodas show the high artistic skills of the Chinese; inscriptions on stone tablets record major events; the ruins of looted imperial gardens bring back sorrowful memories; and the Forbbiden City tells visitors how extravangant the life of emperors had been. One may envision the battle scenes when he stands on the Great Wall. Beijing is like a giant museum of history and a great amusement garden.

We present in this picture book 13 best sights in Beijing, representatives of Beijing's beauty.

天安门

天安门原为明清两代皇城的正门，始建于明永乐15年(1417年)，称"承天门"。历史上曾几次被焚，1651年重修后改称"天安门"。天安门在明清两代是皇帝颁发诏令的地方，每逢冬至皇帝去天坛祭天，夏至到地坛祭地，仲春至先农坛亲耕，皇帝大婚和出兵亲征等重大活动，都要从天安门出入。因此，它的建筑规制甚高，5洞城门，重楼9楹；在中间门洞的前后各立汉白玉石华表一对，华表顶蹲石兽，柱身遍雕祥云腾龙，另有两对石狮前后镇守。新中国成立后，门前左右增设了观礼台，台前置花坛，每当春秋季节，这里花团锦簇，人头攒动，热闹非凡。观礼台前是原皇城的御河——金水河，河上横跨汉白玉石桥5座，桥栏上雕饰着精美的图案和花纹。天安门城楼前是世界上最大的广场——天安门广场。

天安门的设计和建造是一完整的艺术杰作，端庄秀丽，雄伟壮观。1949年10月1日，毛泽东主席在天安门城楼上宣告了中华人民共和国的成立。

Tian'anmen Square

天安门城楼　为重檐庑殿顶，面阔 9 间深
5 间，朱柱黄瓦，美丽壮观。城楼已对公众
开放，登楼远眺，更觉天安门广场宽广博大。

Gate Tower of Tian'anmen   The grand
city gate tower is open to the public. From
it one has a whole view of the Tian'anmen
Square.

Tian'anmen was the front gate of the
Imperial Palace during the Ming and
Qing dynasties. Originally built in 1417
and named Chengtianmen, it was burnt
down and rebuilt several times. The
present gate tower was rebuilt in 1651
and renamed Tian'anmen. Ming and
Qing emperors would issue decrees
from the gate tower and pass through it
when they went to the Temple of Heav-
en in early winter, the Temple of Earth
in early summer and to the Temple of
Agriculture in early spring, or when he
led troops on an expedition. The gate
has five openings and nine tiers of
eaves. Two pairs of white marble pillars stand inside and outside the central opening. Each stone pillar has a
stone beast crowching on top and carvings of clouds and a dragon around it.
There are also two pairs of stone lions
inside and outside of the gate. After the
founding of new China in 1949 reviewing stands were built on the two sides
of the gate. In spring and autumn flowers in front of the reviewing stands at-
tract many visitors. Five white marble
bridges span the Golden Water River
which flows in front of the Tian'anmen.
In front of the gate is the world's largest
open ground in the city -- the Tian'anmen Square.

天安门前华表　在中国古代，华表多设于桥梁、宫殿和城垣前作为装饰和标志。天安门前后的华表是整块汉白玉石雕凿而成的，造型精美，纹饰生动，是华表中的代表作。

Huabiao in front of Tian'anmen In ancient China ornamented stone pillars were often erected by a bridge, palace hall or city wall as an ornament or landmark. The huaobiao in front and behind Tian'anmen were carved out of a whole piece of white marble and bear exquisite carvings in relief. They are the best of huabiao in the country.

天安门广场　是北京的中心广场，面积为44.5公顷。它的北侧屹立着天安门，中央为人民英雄纪念碑，碑南是毛主席纪念堂和正阳门，东西两侧有中国历史博物馆和人民大会堂。广场布局严整，气势宏伟。

Tian'anmen Square　The center of Beijing occupies 44.5 hectares. Tian'anmen stands to its north; the Monument to the People's Heroes rises in the middle; south of the monument are the Memorial Hall of Chairman Mao Zedong and Zhengyangmen Gate; and to the east is the Museum of Chinese History and to its west is the Great Hall of the People.

天安门全景　　**Tian'anmen**

人民英雄纪念碑　建立此碑是为纪念那些自 1840 年以来在争取中华民族独立和自由的斗争中而牺牲了生命的人民英雄。碑身高 37.94 米,碑基占地 3000 平方米。碑正面向着天安门,上有毛泽东主席亲题的"人民英雄永垂不朽"8 个镏金大字,背面是周恩来总理题写的碑文。

Monument to the People's Heroes The monument is dedicated to those who died for the national independence and freedom since 1840. It is 37.94 meters high and occupies an area of 3,000 square meters. On the front side which faces Tian'anmen is eight gilt Chinese characters in Chairman Mao Zedong's handwriting: "People's Heroes Are Immortal". An inscription on the back side is in the handwriting of the late Premier Zhou Enlai.

中国历史博物馆　是与人民大会堂相对称的建筑物,总面积6.9万平方米。馆内收藏和陈列了自170万年前的元谋猿人到1840年前夕的文物资料约30万件,其中大部分为1949年后的考古发掘品,具有极高的历史价值和艺术价值。这里展现的是一部以实物佐证的中华民族的文明发展史。

Museum of Chinese History Directly facing the Great Hall of the People on the eastern side of Tian'anmen Square, the museum on an area of 69,000 square meters keeps 300,000 objects of archaeological finds and cultural relics from the time of Yuanmou Man of 1.7 million years ago to 1840. Greater part of the collection were unearthed after 1949.

人民大会堂　为全国人民代表大会的会址,由万人大会堂、5000人宴会厅和人大常委会办公楼三部分组成,总面积17万多平方米。正门檐部镶嵌着中华人民共和国国徽。整体建筑雄伟庄严,具有民族风格。图为人民大会堂夜景。

Great Hall of the People It serves as the meeting place of the National People's Congress. The immense building is divided into the meeting hall of 10,000 seats, banquet hall for 5,000 guests and offices of the Standing Committee members. It takes up an area of 170,000 square meters. The national emblem hangs above the front gate.

故　宫

　　故宫旧称"紫禁城",是明清两代的皇宫。

　　故宫始建于明永乐 4 年至 18 年(1406－1420 年),后经多次重建与改建,但仍保持原有规模。它占地 72 公顷,由大小数十个院落组成,共有房屋 9000 余间,周围设 10 米高的宫墙和 50 多米宽的护城河,宫墙四隅有角楼,南面正中为午门。故宫主要建筑分外朝和内廷两大部分。外朝以太和、中和、保和三大殿为主体,建在三层汉白玉石台基上,是皇帝行使权力和举行隆重典礼的地方;内廷以乾清宫、交泰殿、坤宁宫为主体,是皇帝处理政务和居住的地方,其两侧东、西六宫为妃嫔的住所。

　　故宫是中国现存规模最大、最完整的皇宫建筑群。整个建筑按中轴线对称布局,主体突出,层次分明,体现了中国古代建筑艺术的优秀传统和独特风格。宫内珍藏有大量的历史文物和艺术品,为中国重点文物保护单位,现为故宫博物院。

Palace Museum

故宫远眺　人们站在景山远眺故宫，但见殿宇重重，金碧辉煌，颇有如临九天神宫，飘飘欲仙的感觉。

The Imperial Palace seen atop Jingshan Hill Golden glazed-tile roofs of the grand halls and towers dazzel the eye in sun light.

Known to many as the Forbbiden City, the Palace Museum was the Imperial Palace of the Ming and Qing dynasties.

The palace was constructed from 1406 to 1420 and has retained the original outlook and scale after many reconstructions and renovations. On its ground of 72 hectares there are several dozen compounds of various sizes with 9,000-odd rooms. The palace is surrounded by a 10-meter-high wall and 50-meter-wide moat. Four towers are located on the four corners of the wall. Wumen (Meridian Gate) is the front gate.

The Imperial Palace is divided into the Outer Palace and Inner Palace. Three main halls in the Outer Palace, Taihe (Supreme Harmony), Zhonghe (Middle Harmony) and Baohe (Preserving Harmony) were where the emperor conducted grand ceremonies. The three halls stand on a white marble terrace of three tiers. The main structures in the Inner Palace are Qianqing (Heavenly Purity) Palace, Jiaotai (Harmoneous Union) Hall and Kunning (Earthly Tranqulity) Palace. The emperor lived and handled state affairs there. The Eastern Palaces and Western Palaces on the two sides were living quarters for imperial consorts.

The Palace Museum is the largest and best preserved imperial building complex in China. Main structures are arranged symmetrically along a central axis in a clear-cut pattern. It keeps a great number of cultural relics and master pieces of art.

午门　是故宫的正门，高 35.6 米，下为高大的砖石墩台，台上有崇楼 5 座，俗称"五凤楼"。午门主楼面阔 9 间，重檐庑殿顶，其两侧设钟鼓亭，每逢朝会和庆典都要击鼓鸣钟，以示威严；战争凯旋，皇帝亲临午门受俘。

Wumen (Meridian Gate) The front gate to the Imperial Palace is 35.6 meters high. Five gate towers rise majestically on a gigantic base of stone and bricks. The main tower with multiple eaves is flanked by a drum pavilion and a bell pavilion. The drum and bell were struck when the emperor gave an audience or appeared at a grand ceremony. As the victorious army returned from a war the emperor would meet it at Wumen and review the captives.

故宫外朝　是故宫最主要的建筑群。从
右至左分别以太和、中和、保和三大殿为核
心，文华、武英二殿为两翼，这里是皇帝举行
大典和召见群臣、行使权力的主要场所。

Outer Palace Taihe, Zhonghe and Baohe
(from right to left) are the main halls in
the Outer Palace. The Wenhua (Glory of
Literature) and Wuying (Militant Grace)
halls are on either side. The Outer Palace
was where the emperor presided major
ceremonies and held audiences.

铜狮　太和门前东、西两侧各有一铜狮,东
雄西雌。雄狮右足踏绣球,象征权力和一统
天下;雌狮左足抚幼狮,象征子嗣昌盛。

Bronze lions On either side of Taihemen
(Gate of Supreme Harmony) is a bronze
lion. The one on the east is male and the
one on the west is female. The male lion
has an embroidered ball under its right
paw to symbolize supreme authority and
the female lion has a cub at her left paw to
symbolize prosperity.

铜龟　太和殿前东、西两端各置一仙鹤和
龟,其背有盖,可燃檀香,烟从嘴逸。鹤龟喻
示长寿。

Bronze turtles On either side of Taihedian
(Hall of Supreme Harmony) are a crane
and a turtle. The turtle has a lid on its back
so that insense sticks could be burnt in its
hollowed body. The aroma would emit
from its mouth. Crane and turtle are sym-
bols for longevity.

太和殿　俗称"金銮殿"。建在高 8.13 米的 3 层汉白玉石台基上,殿高 35.05 米,面宽 11 间,深 5 间,外有廊柱一列,殿内、外立大柱 84 根,飞檐重脊,黄琉璃瓦覆顶,装饰雍容华贵,气势非凡。明清两代皇帝即位、大婚、祝寿以及重大庆典和出兵征讨等活动,都在此举行。

Taihedian (Hall of Supreme Harmony) Popularly known as the Gold Throne Hall, it stands on a white marble terrace of 8.13 meters high and in three tiers. The hall itself is 35.05 meters high. Eighty-four thick wooden pillars are seen in front and inside the hall. The roof is composed of several ridges and multiple eaves covered with golden glazed tiles. Grand ceremonies such as the coronation, wedding and birthday celebration of the emperor and sending off an expedition army were held in this hall.

太和殿内景　殿内面积2377平方米,正中为金漆雕龙宝座和屏风,其两侧有6根沥粉贴金的蟠龙大柱,顶正中为金龙戏珠大藻井,藻井中心倒垂圆球轩辕宝镜,天花板上遍绘玉玺彩画。整个大殿绚丽豪华,金光灿灿,其建筑规格之高,装饰之奢华,堪为中国之最。

Inside Taihedian: The hall has a floor space of 2,377 square meters. A gilt throne is placed in the middle with a screen behind it and six giant pillars decorated with dragons in gold foil on either side. In the center of the caisson ceiling is a design of a golden dragon playing with a pearl. A mirror hangs down from the center of the caisson ceiling. The caisson ceiling is painted in the pattern of the imperial seal. This hall is the mostly extravagantly decorated.

中和殿　位于太和殿后,云亭式建筑。皇帝到太和殿听政前先在此殿小憩,并接受内阁、礼部及侍卫执事等人员的朝拜,然后乘肩舆至太和殿。

Zhonghedian (Hall of Middle Harmony)
Zhonghedian behind the Taihedian was where the emperor took a rest and received greetings of officials from the Cabinet and Protocol Ministry. After that he took a sedan chair to the Taihedian.

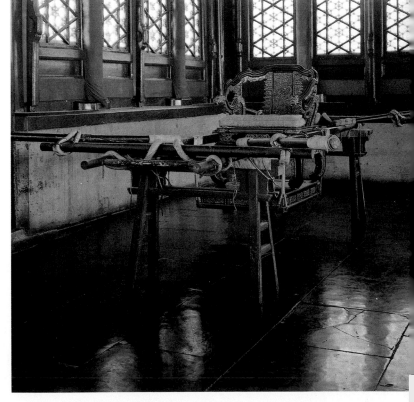

肩舆　俗称轿子,现存于中和殿。它是清代皇帝在宫内使用的交通工具之一。

Sedan chair The sedan chair kept at Zhonghedian was used by emperors of the Qing Dynasty inside the Imperial Palace.

石雕　即云龙阶石御道,嵌于保和殿后基座上。这是一块重 250 吨的整石巨雕,上刻山崖、海水、祥云和 9 条游龙,刻工精细生动。它是明代宫内最大的石雕。

Stone carvings The stone slab in front of the Baohedian bears exquisite carvings of mountain cliffs, flowing water, clouds and nine dragons. Weighing 250 tons, it is the largest piece of stone sculpture of the Ming Dynasty in the Imperial Palace.

乾清宫　为内廷第一座宫殿,这里是明清两代皇帝卧室,也是处理日常政务的殿堂。

Qianqinggong [Palace of Heavenly Purity]: The first palace hall in the Inner Palace was the living quarter of the emperor during the Ming and Qing dynasties. He also did some daily work there.

乾清宫内景　正中为宝座,其上方悬"正大光明"横匾。清代自康熙皇帝以后,在位皇帝生前不宣布皇位继承人,而是将内定的继承人名字写好封于密匣,放置匾后;一旦皇帝驾崩,即当众开匣,宣布皇帝继承人。

Inside Qianqinggong: The throne is placed in the middle of the hall. Above the throne is a horizontal plaque with the characters of "Upright and Honest". Emperor Kang Xi of the Qing Dynasty set the rule that the successor of the emperor was kept in secret. The name of the successor would be written on a piece of paper which was locked in a box and the box would be placed behind the plaque. When the emperor died the box was opened to make the successor known.

乾清宫宝座　这是整体贴金并镶嵌若干红、绿宝石的金椅,其扶手和靠背均由金龙缠绕而成;座后为金漆屏风,屏风正中镌刻着"惟天、惟圣、惟臣、惟民"八个金字,为皇帝的律己格言。

Throne in Qianqinggong The throne is covered with gold leafs and decorated with red and green precious stones. The handles and back are dragons woven with gold thread. On the gold-painted screen behind the throne are the emperor's motto: "Only for Heaven, the Saint, the court officials and the people."

坤宁宫　为明代皇后寝宫,清代改为祭神
场所。据史载,清代康熙、同治、光绪三帝均
在此宫完婚。

Kunninggong (Palace of Earthly Tranquility): During the Ming Dynasty the place was the living quarter of the empress. It became a sacrificial hall during the Qing Dynasty. Emperors Kang Xi, Tong Zhi and Guang Xu of the Qing Dynasty had their wedding ceremonies in this hall.

坤宁宫东暖阁　为皇帝大婚洞房,房内喜床及床上用品为原物;喜床幔帐上绣有几百个活泼可爱的娃娃,这叫作"百子图幔帐",以此祈祝皇帝婚后多子多孙,后继有人。

Eastern Warm Chamber of Kunninggong: It was the nuptial chamber of the emperor. Objects on the bed on display today are originals. Embroidered on the curtain are several hundred lovely babies to predict a thriving royal family.

御花园　是帝、后游幸之所。园内有亭台馆阁 20 余座，山石、花木、盆景点缀其间，各建筑物之间以五色石子甬道相连。花园精巧玲珑，典雅富丽，是中国最具特色的宫廷花园。

Imperial Garden: The Imperial Garden was exclusively reserved for the use of the emperor and his consorts. The two dozen pavilions, towers and halls are surrounded by rockeries, flower beds and miniature landscapes. Paths are paved with pebbles in various designs.

珍妃井　珍妃系光绪皇帝宠妃，因支持皇帝变法维新，触怒慈禧太后而遇害，被太监推入井内溺死，后人将此井名为珍妃井。

Zhen Fei's Well: Zhen Fei, a favorite concubine of Emperor Guang Xu, angered Empress Dowager Ci Xi for she supported the emperor for reform. She was pushed into the well and drowned.

俯瞰角楼 故宫城墙四隅各设一座角楼,它重檐三层,崇脊翘角,俗称"九梁十八柱",精巧玲珑,美丽异常。它体制繁复,协调完美,稳健庄重,集中体现了中国古代建筑的高超技艺和独特风格。

Bird's-eye-view of a corner tower At each of the four corners of the palace wall there is a tower with three layers of flying eaves. The exquisite tower has nine beams and 18 pillars in a steady, harmoneous design. It represents the high artistic style and architectural expertise of ancient China.

神武门　即故宫后门。门楼建在高 10 米的宫墙上,为重檐庑殿式建筑,楼内设钟鼓,楼下宫墙开有三洞券门。清代选秀女、应选女子即由此门进宫。现正中门洞上方嵌有中国文化巨人郭沫若先生书写的"故宫博物院"石匾。

Shenwumen (Gate of Divine Militancy) The rear gate of the Imperial Palace rises above the 10-meter-high wall. Under the roof of multiple eaves there are a bell and drum. During the Qing Dynasty girls were selected to serve in the palace. They would be sent into the palace through this gate. The Chinese characters "The Palace Museum" were written by modern Chinese cultural giant Guo Moruo.

北海公园

北海公园位于北京市中心,面积为70多公顷,其中水面39公顷。北海公园南接中南海,北连什刹海,东与景山公园为邻,东南与故宫相望,山青水秀,景色迷人。

早在公元10世纪,辽代就在这里始建行宫;金代则在这里挖海垒岛,用大批太湖石堆砌假山,起殿筑阁,立坊造栏,建成一座离宫。元代三次扩修这里的琼华岛,并以此为中心建造大都城。明亦大兴土木,在湖滨建五龙亭。清代乾隆年间(1736－1796年),这里连续施工30年,一座规模宏大,设计精巧的皇家园林终臻完整。

北海公园由团城、琼华岛、东岸景区和西北岸景区组成。湖中琼华岛是全园中心,它通过渡船和石桥与其他景区连成一个整体。北海公园布局独特,建筑精美,是北京著名的旅游胜地。

Beihai Park

俯瞰琼华岛　琼岛是北海公园的主体，四面临水，南有永安桥连接团城；湖中菱荷滴翠，碧水映天；岛上万木苍郁，殿阁栉比；巍巍白塔立于琼岛之巅，成为北海公园的标志。

Jionghua Islet The small island is connected with the Circular City by Yong'an Bridge. A giant white dagoba rises on top of it. In summer lotus blossoms bloom in the lake surrounding the island.

The park in the center of Beijing has an area of more than 70 hectares with a water surface of 39 hectares. To its north is Shishahai Lake, to its east is Jingshan Park. The Palace Museum is to its southeast over a short distance.

The imperial court of the Liao Dynasty built a temperory palace on the site of present Beihai Park in the 10th century. During the following Jin Dynasty a lake was dug. The excavated earth was piled to make a hill. Around the lake and on the hill palatial halls, corridors and pavilions were erected. The imperial court of the Yuan Dynasty after the Jin expanded Jionghua Islet in the lake and made it the center of its capital Dadu City. During the Ming Dynasty five pavilions linked with zigzag bridges were built in the northwestern part of the lake. During the reign of Emperor Qian Long (1736-1796) a large-scale project was carried on over 30 years, making the place a grand imperial garden.

Beihai Park is composed of Tuancheng (Circular City), Jionghua Islet, Eastern Shore Scenic Area and Northwestern Shore Scenic Area, with Jionghua Islet as the center. The small island is connected with other parts by a stone bridge and ferry boats.

团城远眺　团城为一砖筑的圆形小城,位于公园南门外。城台高 4.6 米,周长 276 米,台上古木扶疏,殿亭华丽,廊庑曲折,是一处精致的小园林。

Tuancheng (Circular City) The small castle outside the southern gate of Beihai Park was built on a base of 4.6 meters high. It is surrounded by a circular wall of 276 meters long. The seclusive garden is decorated with palatial halls and pavilions and ancient trees.

承光殿　位于城台中央,是团城体量最大的建筑物。其平面为十字形,前后有方形月台,正中为重檐大殿,殿四面均有单檐卷棚式抱厦,顶覆黄琉璃瓦绿剪边,飞檐翘角,宏丽轩昂。明代帝、后常来此观烟火,清代改为佛堂,内供白玉佛。

Chengguang Hall The main structure in the Circular City has a square platform in front and a roof of several tiers of flying eaves. The roof is covered with glazed yellow tiles and edged with green glazed tiles. During the Ming Dynasty the emperor liked to come here to watch fireworks. It was converted into a Buddha hall during the Qing Dynasty. Now there is a Buddha statue of white jade in it.

白玉佛　供于承光殿后厦佛龛内,用整块白玉雕琢而成,高1.5米,顶冠和袈裟饰金箔,并嵌有红绿晶石。佛像肌肤洁白,色泽清润,神态颐静慈祥。1900年八国联军攻入北京,在抢劫北海公园珍宝时,玉佛左臂被砍,至今刀痕尚存。

White jade Buddha The statue in a niche in the rear part of Chengguang Hall is 1.5 meters high. It was carved out of a whole piece of jade. The crown and garment are of gold foil and inlaid with red and green crystals. Its left arm bears gashes made by swords, a result of the looting of soldiers of the Eight-Power Allied Forces who invaded Beijing in 1900.

渎山大玉海　为整玉琢成的大酒缸,俗称玉瓮,重3.5吨,是700多年前的遗物,曾流失,1749年被找回置于玉瓮亭。玉瓮周身刻有精美的出没于海涛中的鱼、龙、海兽,是罕见的文物珍品。

Jade Jar of Dushan Carved out of a whole piece of jade 700 years ago, the jar weighs 3.5 tons. It was lost and retrieved in 1749. It bears exquisite carvings of dragons, water animals and clouds.

白皮古松　相传它曾被乾隆皇帝封为"白袍将军"。它枝繁叶茂,挺拔苍劲,树下是帝、后登城纳凉的佳境。

Lacebark Pine A story tells that Emperor Qian Long conferred on the tree the title of "White-Robed General". The ancient tree is still flourishing.

永安桥　建于13世纪,是连接团城和琼华岛的纽带。桥用汉白玉石砌成,其栏板和望柱分别刻有荷叶和莲花纹;桥两端各立牌坊一座,北为"堆云",南为"积翠",故有"堆云积翠桥"的嘉名。

Yong'an Bridge　The bridge linking the Circular, City and Jionghua Islet was built in the 13th century. Lotus flowers and petals are carved on its balusters and fence boards. Two archways stand on either side of the bridge.

白塔　位于琼华岛之巅,是北海公园最突出的建筑。它始建于 1651 年,后因地震倾圮而重建。这是一座喇嘛塔,高 35.9 米,塔座为折角式须弥座,其上承托覆钵式塔身,正面有门,门内刻有藏文咒语。塔顶有两层铜质伞盖,其边缘悬 14 个铜钟,最上为鎏金火焰宝珠塔刹。

White Dagoba　It was originally built in 1651 but collapsed in an earthquake. The present structure was a later reconstruction. The lamaist dagoda is 35.9 meters high with a tiered base and a body like an upturned bowl. Sutras in Tibetan language are carved inside the front gate. Fourteen copper bells hang from its copper canopy on top of which is a gilt ball like a flame.

善因殿　白塔正南为一组倚山而筑的寺庙建筑群——永安寺,曾是喇嘛烧香礼佛的地方,善因殿为寺的组成部分,位于白塔前,仿木琉璃结构。它面宽4.4米,上圆下方,顶为铜质筒瓦,鎏金宝顶。方形殿的四周墙壁上镶嵌着445尊琉璃佛像。

Shanyin Hall South of the White Dagoda on Qionghua Islet is the Yong'an Temple of Lamasm. The Shanyin Hall, a structure of glazed tiles in imitation of wood, is 4.4 meters wide. The round upper part is topped with a roof of copper tiles and a gilt ball. On the four sides of the square lower part there are 445 Buddhist statues of glazed tiles.

铜仙承露盘　建于琼岛北坡白石平台上,四周玉栏环护,铜仙立于蟠龙石柱顶端,双手托盘,承接甘露。据说清代帝、后常用盘中甘露拌药,意在延年益寿。

Bronze Dew Plate It is placed on a white stone terrace on the northern side of Qionghua Islet guarded by white marble balusters. A bronze immortal purches on top of a stone pillar ornamented with a twining dragon and holds with his hands the dew plate. It is said during the Qing Dynasty the emperor often used the dew collected in the plate to brew his medicine.

延楼长廊　沿琼岛北山麓环湖而建,上下两层。它东起倚晴楼,西止分凉阁,凡60间,长300米,是仿江苏镇江金山江天寺而建的观景廊。

Long Corridor　The 300-meter-long corridor of two layers runs from Yiqing Tower to the east to Fenleng Pavilion to the west. It is a copy of the corridor in the Jiangtian Temple in Zhenjiang, Jiangsu Province. The corridor is a wonderful decoration of the landscape.

画舫斋　为北海东岸主要景区之一。大园林中包含小园林，是清代大型皇家园林的特征之一，被称为"园中之园"。画舫斋就是运用此种造园手法而建造的小园林。这里亭榭环合，游廊曲折，池中鱼戏草动，别有一番情趣。

Huafangzhai During the Qing Dynasty a typical gardening feature was to build smaller gardens inside a large garden. Huafangzhai is a small garden inside Beihai Park on the eastern shore of the lake. The miniature garden is complete with pavilions, corridors, a pool with swimming fish and artificial hills.

远眺北海西北岸景区 从左至右分别为小西天、植物园 (阐福寺)、澄观堂和天王殿, 这些建筑均为严整的中轴对称的几何形布局, 加之五龙亭沿湖点缀, 与自然山水巧妙地融为一体, 颇似一幅不露人工痕迹、宛若天成的"城市山林"风景画。

Northwestern shore of Beihai Lake From left to right are Minor Western Heaven, Botanical Garden (Chanfu Temple), Chengguan Hall and the Hall of Heavenly Kings. These structures are arranged along a central axis in a geometrical pattern. They are blended with the Five-Dragon Pavilions in perfect harmony.

静心斋　是北海公园最著名的园中之园，始建于明代，1759 年扩建，又称乾隆小花园。园中殿堂富丽，斗室幽静，怪石争奇，小溪跌玉，游人置身园中，一步一景，其乐无穷。

Jingxinzhai (Studio of Rested Heart) was built in 1759. Also known as Little Garden of Qian Long, it is the best garden in Beihai Park. The palatial halls, tranquil rooms, rockeries in strange shapes and a stream provide changing sights.

抱素书屋　静心斋内一座相对独立的小院。人们从北海东北方向引来流水，形成泉瀑，水流声如抚琴低吟，又似碧玉落盘，故有韵琴斋之名。抱素书屋为乾隆皇帝及其太子的读书处。

Baosu Shuwu (Study Embracing Books) is a compound in Jingxinzhai Garden. A stream flows from northeast into the compound and creates a small waterfall. The place was used by Emperor Qian Long and his crown son to read.

琉璃阁　　站在静心斋叠翠楼西眺,可望见
一庞大建筑——琉璃阁,其阁顶皆用黄绿琉
璃瓦镶嵌而成,四面墙壁密布琉璃小佛像,
共计 1376 尊。整个建筑巍峨舒展,堂皇富
丽,是北海公园的重要宗教建筑之一。

Liulige Tower Looking west from Diecui
Tower in Jingxinzhai one sees a high structure — the Liulige Tower. The four sides of
the square tower are lined with glazed tiles
and bear 1,376 small Buddha statues, also
made of glazed tiles.

小西天观音殿　小西天又称极乐世界,是乾隆皇帝为其母孝圣皇太后祝寿祈福而修建的;观音殿为中国最大的方亭式宫殿,殿内藻井梁坊上悬"极乐世界"蓝底金字匾,字为乾隆皇帝御笔。

Guanyin Hall of Minor Western Heaven Western Heaven in Buddhism is the Land of Extreme Happiness. Emperor Qian Long built the Guanyin Hall at Minor Western Heaven for his mother to pray for her happiness and longevity. It is the largest palatial hall in the style of a square pavilion in China. A plaque with the characters "Land of Extreme Happiness" in the handwriting of Emperor Qian Long hangs from the ceiling.

五龙亭　始建于 1543 年,五亭中以中亭最大,亭间由白石护栏相连,远看形如游龙。相传这里是帝、后垂钓、观烟火和赏月的地方。

Five-Dragon Pavilions They were built in 1543. The five waterborne pavilions are connected by zigzag bridges. The one in the middle is the largest. In old days the emperor and his consorts came here to fish, watch fireworks or admire the moon.

万佛楼石碑　万佛楼是乾隆皇帝为庆贺其母 80 大寿而建的,楼内墙壁上布满佛龛一万个,每龛一尊金佛像。1900 年八国联军闯进北海,将万尊金佛一抢而空。万佛楼现已无存。此碑系万佛楼落成后修建的,碑高 7.47 米,四面分别用汉、满、蒙、藏四种文字刻乾隆皇帝题写的《万佛楼落成瞻礼诗》。

Stone Tablet in 10,000-Huddha Tower Emperor Qian Long built this tower to celebrate his mother's 80th birthday. Along the walls inside the tower there are 10,000 niches, each used to have a gold Buddha statue. They were all taken away by the soldiers of the Eight-Power Allied Forces who invaded and looted Beijing in 1900. The stone tablet was erected after the tower was completed. It is 7.47 meters high and has an inscription by Emperor Qian Long in four languages of Han, Mongolian, Manchu and Tibetan entitled "Tribute to the Completion of 10,000-Buddha Tower".

九龙壁　建于乾隆 21 年(1756 年),壁高 5
米,厚 1.2 米,长 27 米,整壁用彩色琉璃瓦
镶砌而成,壁两面各有蟠龙 9 条,飞腾戏珠
于波涛云际之中。九龙壁是中国古代琉璃
建筑中的精品。

Nine-Dragon Screen Made in 1756, the
screen wall is five meters high, 1.2 meters
thick and 27 meters long. The whole thing
is built with glazed color bricks. On either
side of it there are nine dragons, also made
of glazed bricks, each playing with a pearl
amidst waves of clouds.

颐和园

颐和园位于北京市西北郊,距市中心约 19 公里,是清代的皇家园林和行宫。

颐和园原名清漪园,建成于 1764 年。它占地 290 公顷,其中水面 220 公顷。园内分为宫廷区、前山前湖区、后山后湖区三大景区,共有殿堂楼阁、亭台水榭 3000 余间,是帝、后政治活动和游憩的地方。1860 年被英法联军焚毁,1888 年慈禧太后挪用海军经费 500 万两白银重建,历时 10 年,竣工后改名"颐和园。"

颐和园北依万寿山,南抱昆明湖,以佛香阁为主体,充分利用地形和水面,从假山的堆造到曲径的走向,从楼阁的配置到花木的点缀,从堤埂的垒砌到亭桥的造型,充分继承和发扬了中国传统的造园技艺,表现出相得益彰的整体园林艺术效果。"虽由人造,宛自天成",素有皇家园林博物馆之称。

Summer Palace

鸟瞰颐和园　万寿山前山以佛香阁和排云殿建筑群为主体,其他各建筑物自由地、疏朗地布置在山麓、山坡或山脊上,以此烘托主体建筑的端庄、华丽;昆明湖于山前展开,碧水荡漾,幽深静谧。整体布局重点突出,主宾分明,既体现了皇家园林雍容磅礴的气势,又不失其婉约清丽的风姿。

Bird's-eye view of the Summer Palace　The Foxiang Tower and Paiyun (Dispursing Clouds) Hall rise majestically on top of the hill. Other structures are scattered in a seemingly random way on the hill to enhance the majesty of the two main buildings. In front of the hill Kunming Lake stretches out like a mirror. There is an atmosphere of imperial dignity and an air of leisure of a garden.

The Summer Palace lies 19 kilometers northwest from Beijing downtown area. It used to be an imperial garden and temporary palace during the Qing Dynasty (1664-1911).

Originally named Qingyiyuan, the Summer Palace was built in 1764. It has a total area of 290 hectares with a water surface of 220 hectares, and is divided into three scenic areas: one of the imperial court, one in front the hill and one behind the hill. British and French soldiers invaded Beijing in 1860 and looted the Summer Palace. Many precious objects were taken away and buildings burnt down. In 1888 Empress Dowager Ci Xi rebuilt the imperial garden with 5 million taels of silver budgeted for the Imperial Navy. The reconstruction was completed in ten years.

The Longevity Hill rises on the northern shore of Kunming Lake. Foxiang (Buddha Fragrance) Tower dominates the hill. Scattered on the hill and around the lake are individual gardens, palatial halls and towers, painted corridors, bridges and a great variety of plants. The Summer Palace is the cream of Chinese traditional gardening art.

东宫门　颐和园正门,门为三明两暗的庑殿式建筑,中间正门供帝、后出入,称为"御路",两边门洞供王公大臣出入,太监、兵卒从南北两侧边门出入。匾额"颐和园"三字为光绪皇帝御题。云龙石刻有二龙戏珠浮雕;龙为皇家尊严的象征,又是谕旨和敕令的标志。

Eastern Palace Gate It is the main entrance to the Summer Palace. The opening in the center was for the emperor and empress exclusively. The two side openings were for the use of princes and court officials. Eunuchs and soldiers used side gates to the south and north. The name plaque "Yiheyuan" in front of the gate was written by Emperor Guang Xu. The stone slab in front of the gate bears a carving in relief of two dragons playing with a pearl, a symbol of imperial authority.

仁寿殿　是宫廷区的主要建筑之一,原名勤政殿,光绪年间改为今名,意为施仁政者长寿。它是清朝末年慈禧太后和光绪皇帝听政的大殿,也是中国近代史上变法维新运动的策划地之一。1898年光绪皇帝曾在此殿召见改良派领袖康有为,任命他为总理各国事务衙门章京上行走,准其专褶奏事,从而揭开了维新变法的序幕。但好景不长,由于封建保守势力的反对,"百日维新"终归失败。

Renshou (Benevolence and Longevity) Hall It was originally named Qinzheng (Be Diligent in Administration). The present name came into being during the reign of Emperor Guang Xu. It was used by Empress Dowager Ci Xi and Emperor Guang Xu to give audiences. In 1898 Emperor Guang Xu met Kang Youwei, leader of the reformists, in this hall and appointed him a high-ranking court minister. But the reform failed in 100 days because the conservative force was too strong.

乐寿堂　为一大型四合院,慈禧太后的寝宫。大殿红柱灰顶,垂脊卷棚歇山式,造型别致,富丽堂皇。

Leshou (Happy Longevity) Hall The large courtyard was the living quarters of Empress Dowager Ci Xi. The red pillars and gray gabled roof display a unique style of architecture.

大戏楼　建于大型院落"德和园"内,是中国现存最大的古戏楼,它高 21 米,分上中下三层。下层天花板中心有天井与上层戏台串通,中层戏台设有绞车,可巧设机关布景,上天入地,变化无穷。

Grand Opera Tower The imperial theater in the Dehe Garden is the largest of its kind in China today. It is 21 meters high and has three floors. An opening is in the ceiling of the first floor, in which a winch could lower performers and props down onto the first floor. Performers could appear on the three floors at the same time.

慈禧太后画像　慈禧姓叶赫那拉,是清代第七位皇帝咸丰(公元 1851－1861 年在位)的贵妃,咸丰死后,她在"垂帘听政"的名义下独揽朝纲达 48 年之久。1905 年荷兰画家华士·胡博(Hubert Vos)应邀为慈禧太后画像,是年她年逾七旬。画像现存德和园内。

Portrait of Empress Dowager Ci Xi Ci Xi, a concubine of Xian Feng, the seventh emperor of the Qing Dynasty (reigned between 1851 and 1861). After the emperor died she took over the power to "rule behind the curtain" for 48 years. The portrait was made by Dr. Hubert Vos of Holland when the dowager was already more than 70 years old. It is kept in Dehe Garden.

从西堤看万寿山

Longevity Hill seen from the western shore of Kunming Lake.

长廊　东起邀月门，西止石丈亭，全长 728 米，共 273 间画廊，是中国廊建筑中最大、最长、最负盛名的长廊。

Long Corridor The 728-meter-long corridor runs from a moon gate in the east to Shizhang Pavilion in the west. All the 273 sections are painted with pictures either of ancient stories or landscapes. It is the longest and most famous corridor in China.

长廊彩画 彩画题材十分广泛，有花鸟、树石、山水、人物等。18 世纪中叶，乾隆皇帝（公元 1736 －1795 年在位）曾派宫廷画师到杭州西湖写生，得西湖景 546 幅，这些湖景被悉数移绘到长廊 273 间画廊的梁枋上。本世纪 60 年代，中国政府不仅保留了西湖风景画，还增绘了具有民族特色的彩画 14000多幅，使长廊成为名副其实的画廊。图为中国神话小说《西游记》中"孙悟空大闹天宫"的故事。

Pictures on the Long Corridor Paintings on the Long Corridor depict a broad range of subject matter such as flowers, birds, trees, rockeries, landscapes and human figuers. Emperor Qian Long (1736-1795) sent court painters to sketch scenic spots around West Lake in Hangzhou. They brought back 546 pictures, which they transferred onto the wooden boards betwen rafters and pillars in the Long Corridor. In the 1960s 14,000 pictures of other subjects were added to the original ones. This picture is about the Monkey King Making Hovac in Heaven, an episode from the classic novel *Pilgrimage to the West*.

排云殿　万寿山前山主体建筑之一，是专门为慈禧太后过生日受贺而建的大殿。大殿横列复道与左右耳殿相连，共有房屋 21 间，均为朱柱黄瓦，金龙眩目，气势宏大。

Paiyun (Dispursing Clouds) Hall One of the main buildings on the Longevity Hill, it was specially built for Empress Dowager Ci Xi to receive her birthday greetings. Corridors link the main hall to side houses on both sides. Pillars in crimson color and the roof with golden glazed tiles dazzle brightly in sunshine.

佛香阁　建于万寿山前山陡坡高 21 米的巨石台基上。它南对昆明湖，背靠智慧海佛殿，以它为中心的各建筑群严整而对称地向两翼展开，彼此呼应，蔚为壮观。1860 年佛香阁被英法联军烧毁，后照原样重建，是座宗教建筑。

Foxiang (Buddha Fragrance) Tower It stands on a 21-meter-high stone terrace on the sheer front side of the Longevity Hill. It overlooks Kunming Lake in front and Zhihuihai Buddha Hall in the back. Other buildings stretch on either side of it in a neat symmetrical pattern. The tower was burnt down by British and French soldiers in 1860 and a new one was built on the site later.

清晏舫　又名石舫,建于1755年,舫身用巨石雕造而成。通长36米,有上下两层舱房。取意"水能载舟,亦能覆舟",喻示清王朝坚如磐石,水不能覆。

Qingyanfang Also known as Stone Boat, it was made with huge stone blocks in 1755. The 36-meter-long immovable boat has two tiers. It was placed in the lake to symbolize the steadfast rule of the Qing Dynasty.

宝云阁　俗称铜亭,内供佛像,曾两次遭浩劫,佛像和亭的部分构件被偷运海外。铜亭铸于1752年,高7.55米,重207吨。据史料记载,铸造时,仅磨凿下的铜屑就重2.5吨。铜亭为重檐方顶,亭身的菱花隔扇、柱、梁、斗拱、椽、瓦以及九龙匾、对联等,都同木结构一模一样,通体呈蟹青冷古铜色。铜亭造型精美,是世界上罕见的青铜建筑精品。

Baoyun [Precious Cloud] Tower Popularly known as the Copper Pavilion, it was cast in 1752 with 207 tons of copper. It is said five tons of coppy dust was collected during polishing the structure. The square roof has several tiers of eaves and latticed windows. The pillars, rafters, rackets, tiles and beams are all in imitation of wood, giving a cold seasoned luster.

昆明湖西堤　是仿杭州西湖苏堤而建造的。堤上除 6 座小桥外，没有任何高大建筑，显得深邃沉静，与万寿山前山热烈浓密的风景区形成强烈的景观对比效果。

Western shore of Kunming Lake It is a copy of the Su Causeway at West Lake in Hangzhou. Along the shore there are no man-made objects except six bridges. The quietness there is a strong contrast with the bustling area in front of the Longevity Hill.

知春亭　位于昆明湖东堤。四面环水，亭畔点缀山石，种植桃柳。冬去春来湖水最早在这里消融，告知人们：春天已经来临。

Zhichun (Be Aware of Spring) Pavilion The pavilion on the eastern shore of Kunming Lake is surrounded by water and decorated with rockeries and peach and willow trees. In early spring the ice in the lake begins to melt from here to harbinger the spring.

铜牛　铸造于1755年。它两角耸立,双耳竖起,目光炯炯,形象逼真。牛背上铸有80字篆体铭文,说明它是用来镇水的。

Bronze Bull Cast in 1755 the bull has upturned horns and ears. Its eyes look intensively ahead. A note of 80 characters inscribed on its body tells that it was used to suppress flood.

十七孔桥　是昆明湖东堤连接湖心南湖岛的巨型石桥,全长150米。桥头和桥栏望柱上共雕有544只石狮,其形态无一雷同。

17-Arch Bridge The 150-meter-long stone bridge links the South Islet with the eastern shore of Kunming Lake. On the heads of balusters of the bridge there are 544 stone lions of various postures and looks.

谐趣园　位于万寿山后山东麓,是颐和园的"园中之园"。它是仿江南名园——无锡寄畅园而修建的。园内有 5 处轩堂,7 座亭榭,百间游廊,5 座小桥。所有建筑环绕荷池展开,极富江南园林柔媚清秀的特色。

Xuequ (Harmoneous Interest) Garden Located on the eastern part of the back of the Longevity Hill, the garden is an imitation of Jichang Garden in Wuxi City. It has five halls, seven pavilions, several corridors and five small bridges on a lotus pond. It is well known for the exquisiteness, typical to gardens south of the Yangtze River.

四大部洲 是万寿山后山的主体建筑。原建筑是藏式香严宗印之阁，象征佛教中的须弥山。1860 年毁于战火，光绪年间重修时主殿改为佛殿，内供佛像。

Four Great Lands This main group of buildings on the back of the Longevity Hill was devoted to Tibetan Buddhism. It was detroyed in 1860. When it was rebuilt in the reign of Emperor Guang Xu, the main hall was changed to worship the Buddha.

苏州街　位于颐和园后湖中段，街道蜿蜒曲折 300 余米，建筑面积近 3000 平方米。列肆于宫苑，始于汉代（公元前 206－公元 220 年）。苏州街和它上方的四大部洲寺庙群形成了"以庙带肆"的商业模式。它以水当街，以岸作市，共有 64 座铺面，14 座牌楼、牌坊，8 座小桥。这里的店铺，多为民间老字号名店，所列商品并不真的出售，仅为点缀街面，造成一种热闹气氛。

Suzhou Street The street runs 300 meters along the shore of Rear Lake behind the Longevity Hill and covers an area of 3,000 square meters. First buildings appeared along the street during the Han Dynasty (206 B.C.-220 A.D.) There used to be 64 stores, 14 archways and eight bridges. The once busy commercial street has been restored as a tourist attraction in the Summer Palace.

天　坛

　　天坛是明、清两代皇帝祭天的场所。据史载,郊祀天地,周代已成大典,汉、唐(公元 618－907 年)以后相沿成制。十五世纪初,明代建成天地坛合祭天地,中叶实行四郊分祀天地日月之制,此处专供祭天,所以名天坛。清代予以扩建,成为中国现存规模最大的坛庙建筑群。

　　天坛占地 273 公顷,建筑布局呈"回"字形,由两道坛墙构成内坛、外坛两大部分。外坛墙总长 6416 米,内坛墙总长 3292 米。内外坛墙的北部呈半圆形,南部为方形,北高南低,这既表示天高地低,又表示"天圆地方"。天坛的主要建筑物集中在内坛中轴线的南北两端,其间由一条宽阔的丹陛桥相连结,由南至北分别为圜丘坛、皇穹宇、祈年殿和皇乾殿等;另有神厨、宰牲亭和斋宫等建筑和古迹。

　　天坛设计巧妙,色彩调和,建筑艺术高超,是中国非常出色的古建筑之一。

The Temple of Heaven

天坛全景　主要建筑物集中在内坛中轴线，由上至下分别为祈年殿、皇穹宇和圜丘坛。

The Temple of Heaven The main buildings on a central axis (from top to buttom): Hall of Prayer for Good Harvest, Imperial Vault of Heaven and Circular Mound Altar.

During the Ming and Qing dynasties, the emperor came to the Temple of Heaven to pay homage to Heaven. The custom to worship Heaven and the earth came into being during the Zhou Dynasty (c. 11th century-256 B.C.) and elaborated into a formal ritual during the Han and Tang dynasties (618-907). In the early 15th century a temple was built to pay respect to both heaven and the earth and in the middle of that century the ceremonies to worship heaven, the earth, the sun and the moon were conducted at four seperate temples. The Temple of Heaven was expanded during the Qing Dynasty and has remained as the largest complex of temples in China.

The Temple of Heaven has an area of 273 hectares with a layout in two squares one inside the other. Two walls divide the ground into the outer and inner parts. The outer wall is 6,416 meters long and the inner wall is 3,292 meters long. The northern part of the outer and inner walls is a semicircle and the southern part of them is square, declining from north to south to symbolize the traditional belief that Heaven was high and round and the earth was low and rectangular. Main structures are located on the ends of a flagstone-paved central north-south path: from south to north are the Circular Mound Altar, Imperial Vault of Heaven, the Hall of Prayer for Good Harvest and Huangqian Hall. Auxiliary structures include Divine Kitchen, Slaughter Pavilion and Palace of Abstinence.

The Temple of Heaven is an outstanding representative of Chinese traditional architecture for its clever design and harmoneous colors.

俯瞰斋宫 斋宫占地 4 万平方米,坐西朝东,呈正方形。宫内主要建筑有正殿、寝宫、钟楼等,共有房屋 60 余间,人称"小皇宫"。这里是皇帝祭天、祈谷前斋戒、沐浴的寝宫。

A bird's-eye view of the Palace of Abstinence The square compound on an area of 40,000 square meters has a main hall, living quarters for the emperor and a drum tower. The emperor fasted and took a bath before he started the ceremony to pay homage to heaven.

斋宫正殿　汉白玉石殿基,庑殿顶,5开间,系砖券结构,不设梁柱,故又名无梁殿。殿前月台上建有铜人石亭和石辰亭。

Main hall of the Palace of Abstinence The hall on a white marble foundation is of bricks without any pillar or beam. Bronze statues, a stone pavilion and a stone pavilion with a sundial are in front of the hall.

正殿内景　是皇帝斋戒期间接见群臣的地方。殿内端坐者是清代乾隆皇帝的蜡像。他身着朝袍,栩栩如生。

Inside the main hall The emperor used the hall to receive court officials. The seated wax statue is of Emperor Qian Long of the Qing Dynasty.

正殿左厅　厅内陈列的是皇帝祭天时使用的编磬、乐钟和祭器。

Left parlor of the main hall Displayed in this room are a set of jade chimes, musical bells and sacrificial objects used by the emperor for the ceremony.

鸟瞰祈年殿　从左至右分别为皇乾殿、祈谷坛、东西配殿和祈年门。所有建筑由一方形围墙围成院落。俯视其景，"白玉高坛紫翠重，不是天宫似天宫"。

A bird's-eye view of the Hall of Prayer for Good Harvest From left to right within a rectangular wall are the Huangqian Hall, Qigu Terrace, eastern and western wing halls and the Gate of Prayer for Good Harvest.

祈年门　位于祈年殿正南,为5开间大宫门,上盖兰色琉璃瓦,下承白石崇基。它曾先后被命名为大祀门和大享门。

Gate of Prayer for Good Harvest The grand gate south of the Hall of Prayer for Good Harvest stands on a white marble base and has a roof of blue glazed tiles. It was once named Daji and Daheng at different times.

祈年殿　又称祈谷殿,是明清两代皇帝孟春祈谷之地。其构造形式为上屋下坛,三层屋檐层层收缩,作伞状。殿高32米,底部直径24.2米,巍然屹立于6米高的汉白玉圆台上,大有拔地擎天之势,恢弘壮观,气势非凡。

Hall of Prayer for Good Harvest Also known as Qigu Hall, it was the spot where the emperor of the Ming and Qing dynasties prayed for good harvest in spring. The umbrella-like structure of three tiers stands on a six-meter-high white marble circular terrace and is 32 meters high and 24.2 meters around at the base.

祈年殿内景　祈年殿是按"敬天礼神"的思想设计的,殿内立柱都有特定的寓意:里层4根龙井柱间的空间象征春夏秋冬四季;中层12根朱红柱分割的空间象征一年的12个月;外层12根檐柱象征一天的12个时辰;宝顶下的雷公柱象征皇帝的"一统天下"。

Inside the Hall of Prayer for Good Harvest
The pillars inside the hall all have a meaning: the four in the inner circle represent the four seasons of the year; the 12 pillars in the middle circle represent 12 months of the year and the 12 pillars in the outer circle represent 12 time periods of the day. The Leigong Pillar under the center of the ceiling means the absolute power of the emperor.

丹陛桥　是连接祈年殿和皇穹宇的南北大道,长360米、宽29.4米,因道下有一隧洞与其交叉,故名桥。桥南端高约1米,北端高约4米,由南向北逐渐升高,象征皇帝步步登高,寓升天之意。由于是升天之路,所以又叫"神道"。神道两侧左为"御道",右为"王道"。天帝神灵走神道,皇帝走御道,王公大臣走王道。

Danbi Bridge It is actually the main road in the Temple of Heaven between the Hall of Prayer for Good Harvest and Imperial Vault of Heaven. It is 360 meters long and 29.4 meters wide. A tunnel passes through under the path, so it is called a bridge. The southern end of the road is one meter above the ground and the northern end of it is four meters above the ground. The rise meant to "step upward toward heaven". The central path was reserved for divine gods; the path on the left was reserved for the emperor and the path on the right was used by court officials.

琉璃门　为皇穹宇正门，庑殿式建筑，筒瓦及斗拱均为琉璃制品，这在北京古建筑中尚不多见。

Glazed Tile Gate　The front gate of the Imperial Vault of Heaven is made entirely of glazed bricks and tiles, a rare piece of architecture among ancient buildings in Beijing.

皇穹宇　是专门安放神牌的殿宇,俗称寝宫。它高 19.5 米,底部直径 15.6 米,全木结构,殿顶由 8 根立柱支撑,顶无横梁,由众多斗拱上叠,天花板层层收缩,构成美丽的穹窿式藻井。此殿构筑精美别致,挺拔舒展,令人赏心悦目。

Imperial Vault of Heaven The place was used to keep wooden tablets for worship. It is 19.5 meters high and 15.6 meters around at the base. Built entirely of wood, the vault is supported by eight pillars. The roof has no beams but only a great number of brackets intwined within each other. The ceiling tapers upward to form a beautiful caisson.

回音壁　即皇穹宇围墙,呈圆形,周长193.2米,高3.7米,厚0.9米。它是一堵磨砖对缝的围墙,若两人面壁分别站在东西墙根,一人对墙低声说话,声波沿墙壁连续反射前进,另一个可以清晰听见。

Echo Wall The circular wall surrounding the Imperial Vault of Heaven is 193.2 meters long, 3.7 meters high and 0.9 meter thick. If one speaks against the wall at one end another can hear his voice at the other end of it.

三音石　即皇穹宇殿前御道上的第三块石板。人们若敞开殿门,关紧窗,站在石板上拍一掌或喊一声,可听到三声或更多声的回音。这是因为第三块石板位于圆形围墙的中心,声波从这里发出几乎同时经圆形墙壁返回,如此反复,即可听到多次回音。但在帝王时代,这被蒙上了神秘的色彩,说是"人间私语,天闻若雷"。据此,第三块石板又被称为"天闻若雷石"。

Three-Echoes Stone It is the third stone slab on the path in front of the Imperial Vault of Heaven. When one stands on it and claps his hands three or more echoes seem to emit from the stone. It can cause such echoes because it is located in the middle under the Echo Wall. It was made mysterious in the old days by the rulers to prevent gossiping against them.

圜丘坛　俗称祭天台,是一座由汉白玉石雕栏围绕的三层石造圆台,通高 5 米余,洁白如玉,极为壮观。明清两代,每年冬至日皇帝亲临此坛祭天,这既是感谢皇天上帝赐给的年丰政和,又是祈求来年的国泰民安。

Circular Mound Altar Also known Heaven Mound Altar, it is five meters high and of three tiers. Around each tier there are white marble balusters. During the Ming and Qing dynasties in early winter the emperor would come to this mound to pay homage to heaven and pray for peace and a good harvest.

天心石　即圜丘坛上层坛面的中心石。从中心石向外,每层有 9 环扇形石板,每环依次加 9 块,共 3402 块。它们大小一致,形状相同,安装严丝合缝,虽经数百年风雨侵蚀,依然平整如初。当人们站在天心石上轻唤一声,可马上听到响亮回音,这是中国建筑史上的奇迹。

Heart of Heavenly Stone The stone placed in the center of the top tier of the Circular Mound Altar. Around it there are nine circles, each with nine stones, altogether 3,402 pieces. They are of identical size and appearance and put closely together. They have remained intact during the past several hundred years. When people stand on the Heart of Heavenly Stone and shout echoes will be heard.

长廊　共72间,呈"W"形,是祭祀时运送祭品的廊道。原为通脊连檐,前有窗,后有墙,故又名七十二连房。

Long Corridor The corridor in the pattern of a "W" has 72 sections. It was used to deliver sacrificial objects during the ceremony to pay homage to heaven.

宰牲亭　　在长廊的最东端，高垣一重，另
成一院，有独门与长廊相连。祭祀用的牛、
羊、猪、鹿、兔等均在这里宰杀。

Slaughter Pavilion It is in a seperate compound at the eastern end of the Long Corridor. Before a ritual, cattle, sheep, pigs,
deer and rabits were killed here as sacrif-
ices.

甘泉井　位于神厨院内,水清甘冽,祭天的供馔和太羹均用此水调制。明代的道士们说,此井通天,是天河之水。明皇朱厚熜信以为真,赐名"天泉"。

Sweet Spring Well　The water from the well in the compound of the Divine Kitchen tastes sweet. It was used to make soup for the sacrificial ritual. Taoists in the Ming Dynasty said the well was connected with heaven. Emperor Zhu Houzong believed it and named the well "Heavenly Well".

双环万寿亭 位于祈年殿西侧柏林中。公元 1741 年,乾隆皇帝为其母庆祝 50 大寿,在中南海修建此亭。1977 年从原址迁到这里。双环亭为两个圆亭套合而成,造型新颖,是木构架建筑中的奇葩。

Double-Circle Longevity Pavilion The pavilion was originally built in 1741 by Emperor Qian Long to celebrate his mother's 50th birthday in the Imperial Palace. In 1977 it was relocated in a cypress grove on the western side of the Hall of Prayer for Good Harvest. It is a master piece of wooden structures from ancient times.

九龙柏 生长于回音壁墙外,相传是明永乐年间栽植的,距今已有 500 多年历史。因树干扭结纠缠,恰似九龙盘旋,故名九龙柏。

Nine-Dragon Cypress The tree outside the Echo Wall was planted 500 years ago. Its twining branches look like nine dragons.

圆明园遗址公园

　　圆明园位于北京西北郊，始建于1709 年，由圆明、长春、绮春三园组成，统称圆明园，占地 350 公顷。它是经清朝五代皇帝倾全国物力、集无数巧匠在 150 年间相继建成的一座大型皇家宫苑；是中国古典园林艺术的杰出典范，名闻天下，被誉为"万园之园"。

　　园内集东西方风格的名胜凡 40 景，大型建筑 145 处。其中有中国传统的江南园林式建筑群，有欧洲风格的宫廷区。它们或建于湖岸，或掩映于绿荫，或立于山丘，画栋雕梁，典雅秀丽，气象万千。园内具有江南水乡地貌的福海水系，萦绕于三园丘山之间，彼此沟通，烟水迷离，极富诗情画意。

　　圆明园还是当时中国收藏珍宝、文物和图书的皇家博物馆，堪称中国传统文化精品的宝库。

　　不幸的是，这一被称为"人类一大奇迹"的艺术杰作分别于 1860 年、1900 年遭英法联军、八国联军劫掠焚毁，化为废墟，实为人类历史上的一大劫难。现在园林格局依存，经过整修的圆明园遗址已成为人民群众和中外游客凭吊游览的一个重要景点。

Yuanmingyuan (Old Summer Palace)

绮春园大门　门为五楹歇山庑殿式，其左右为影壁，门前列双狮。此门现为圆明园正门。

Front gate of Yichun Garden On either side of the gate is a screen wall and in front of it there are two stone lions.

Construction of Yuanmingyuan, the Old Summer Palace, began in 1709 and continued for 150 years. It was once known as "Leader of the gardens in the world".

The whole ground of 350 hectares was made up with three gardens: Yuan-ming (Round and Bright), Changchun (Everlasting Spring) and Yichun (Exquisite Spring). Forty scenic spots and 145 architectural objects followed both European and Chinese styles. There was an area built in imitation of an European palace. Painted pavilions, towers and corridors were seen along the shores of lakes, in trees or on hills. A stream flew through the three gardens. Yuanmingyuan was also the imperial museum with numerous precious articles, cultural relics and books.

But the marvelous man-made wonder was detroyed by British and French soldiers in 1860 and by soldiers of the Eight-Power Allied Forces in 1900. It was only recently restored in part and has become a favorite tourist attraction in Beijing.

鑑碧亭　位于绮春园西部,座落在湖心一座正方形孤岛上,须渡舟才能登上亭台。原亭端庄秀丽,雕梁画栋。图为正在修复中的鑑碧亭。

Jianbi Pavilion Located on a square small island in the center of the lake, it can be reached only by boat. The pavilion is being restored to its original grandeur.

海宴堂　是西洋楼区规模最大的一座楼房。建筑西向,楼前有一喷水池,池边列八字形石台,台上分列兽头人身十二生肖,昼夜依次轮流喷水一个时辰,正午喷齐,俗称"水利钟"。1860 年遭英法联军焚毁,成为一片废墟。

Haiyan Hall It is the largest of Eureapon-style buildings in Yuanmingyuan. There used to be a fountain in front of the building. On a long stone platform were 12 stone animals spurting water in rotation, each for two hours. At noon all of them would emit water. The whole project was called a "water clock". It was totally destroyed by British and French soldiers in 1860.

方外观(五竹亭) 是一座清真寺,曾是乾隆皇帝的爱妃香妃(即容妃)做礼拜的地方。英法联军破坏后,仅剩下孤零零几个石柱。

Fangwai Temple (Wuzhu Pavilion) It was a mosque built by Emperor Qian Long for his favorite concubine Xiang Fei who was a moslem. Only a few stone pillars have been left from the looting in 1860.

大水法　是由喷水池、壁龛式屏风和一对水塔组成的喷泉，为当时西洋楼区最宏丽的景观。中部水池有一组生动逼真的"十狗逐鹿"雕塑。当所有喷泉一齐喷射时，水声可传几公里之远。

Dashuifa It was composed of a fountain, a screen and two water towers, the most magnificent sight in the European area of Yuanmingyuan. When the "Ten Dogs Chasing a Deer", a group of sculptures in the fountain, spurted water, the sound could be heard several kilometers away.

远瀛观　建于西洋楼区中心，曾作为香妃的住所。目前，遗址上保存下来的门柱雕刻精美、花纹绮丽，通过它可见当年手工艺人的高超技艺。图为月夜中的远瀛观遗址。

Yuanying Temple The temple in the middle of the European building group was a residence of Xiang Fei, a concubine of Emperor Qian Long. Carvings on the remanent gate pillars show the high level of ancient Chinese craftsmen. The picture was taken at a moonlit night.

万花阵　　是摹仿欧洲皇家花园中的迷宫而建的，宽 60 米、长 90 米、高 1.5 米。阵中心有一座汉白玉石亭。每年中秋之夜皇帝命宫女头顶黄绸纱灯随意穿行，以欣赏流动奔走的灯影，故又称"黄花灯"。万花阵毁于第二次鸦片战争。现已照原模式修复。

Wanhuazhen (10,000-Flower Formation) A copy of a labyrinth of an imperial garden in Europe, it is 60 meters wide, 90 meters long and 1.5 meters high. A white marble pavilion rises in the center of the formation. In the middle of autumn the emperor would order court female servants to walk around in the formation with a silk lantern on each's head for him to enjoy. It was destroyed in 1880 in the second Opium War. The present formation is a recent reconstruction.

福海　在圆明园三园的中心，水面约 35 公顷。福海中心的三岛称"蓬岛瑶台"，象征东海蓬莱、方丈、瀛州三仙山，是帝王们追求人间仙境，长生不老的一种幻想境界。福海是园内大型水上娱乐场所，当时每逢端午节在此举行龙舟竞渡活动。经修整，它的山形水系已复原貌，部分亭台轩榭已重建。

Fuhai (Sea of Happiness) Located at the joint spot of the three gardens of Yuanmingyuan, it has a water surface of 35 hectares. The three small islands in the water have the names of three fairy islands where immortals lived: Penglai, Fangzhang and Yingzhou. It has been made into a waterborne amusement ground. In early autumn a dragon boat race is held on the lake. The water system has been restored and some pavilions built according to the original design.

西峰秀色遗址　原是一个花架作门、花篱作墙的庭院。它的主体建筑"含韵斋",曾是雍正皇帝的住所。因可观赏到几十里外的西山群峰,故命名"西峰秀色",为园内四十景之一。现在一片狼藉,面目全非。

Site of Xifeng Xiuse Xifeng Xiuse (Beauty of Western Peak) was originally a courtyard with flower trellises as the gate and wall. Hanyun Studio, its main structure, was a bedroom of Emperor Yong Zheng. From there one could see the Western Mountains a dozen kilometers away. It was reduced to desolation.

紫碧山房遗址　位于圆明园西部,是全园最高点。登高远望,全园景色尽收眼底。原来辉煌的殿宇,现在已成为碎石荒岗。

Site of Zibi Mountain Villa The site in the western part is the highest point of Yuanmingyuan. There used to be palatial halls but now all in ruins.

大观园

　　大观园位于北京市西南隅的护城河畔，原址为明清两代皇家菜园。大观园占地13万平方米，其中水面2.4万平方米。园内有庭院楼阁、亭台水榭数百间，是一座典型的清代官家园林。

　　大观园是北京市有关部门于80年代中期依据中国著名古典小说《红楼梦》所描述的场景而建造的。《红楼梦》主要通过贾宝玉、林黛玉和薛宝钗三人之间的爱情纠葛及其不幸结局，反映了18世纪中国封建贵族的兴衰史。园内建筑采用中国古典建筑技法和传统的造园技艺，忠实于原著描绘的时代风尚，从花草树木的栽植，山形水系的设计以及室内陈设和人物雕塑，无不体现18世纪的风情和习俗。人们漫步园中，耳畔萦绕着哀伤的《红楼梦》古曲，使人触景生情，引发怀古幽思。

Grand-View Garden

大观园正门 为五开间庑殿式门，坐北朝南，双石狮镇守左右。秉门正看，它齐檐立柱，雕梁画栋，灰色筒瓦覆顶，精雕图案饰于门栏窗棂，门前为白石台阶，两边是一色水磨"八"字影壁墙。整个门面端庄典雅，威严气派。

Front gate of Grand-View Garden It faces south and has two stone lions as its guards. The pillars and windows are elaborately painted and carved. The steps in front of the gate are of white marble. Two screen walls on either side of the gate are built with polished bricks.

Grand-View Garden was built on the site of an imperial vegetable garden in southwestern suburbs during the Ming and Qing dynasties. Downtown Beijing has long been expanded over it. The garden has an area of 130,000 square meters with a water surface of 24,000 square meters. Following the style of imperial gardens of the Qing Dynasty, it has several hundred houses, waterside pavilions and towers.

In the mid-1980s Beijing decided to build a garden according to the description of the Grand-View Garden in the classical novel *A Dream of Red Mansions*. The novel, through a love story between Jia Baoyu and the two girls of Lin Daiyu and Xue Baochai, tells the decline of an aristcratic family in the 18th century. The designers of the garden followed truthfully the customs of that time in the construction of buildings, the planting of trees and flowers and the making of statues of characters from the novel.

省亲别墅　是接待皇妃贾元春的行宫,由前后两个院落组成。这里崇阁巍峨,玉栏绕砌,建筑与装饰仿皇家规制,恢弘壮观且奢华异常。

House of Reunion　The compound in the novel was for Imperial Consort Jia Yuanchun to stay when she returned home from the palace. The houses are high and surrounded with white marble balusters to display the extravagance of the royal family.

顾恩思义殿　元妃省亲入园后,在此殿升座受礼,大开筵宴。据小说描述,殿前"顾恩思义"匾额和两旁的柱联为元妃所题。此殿是大观园中气势最磅礴的殿堂。

Hall of Gratitude　When Imperial Consort Jia Yuanchun visited her family she received the greetings and entertained her family with a grand banquet in this hall. The inscriptions on the name plaque and a couplet on the pillars are in the handwriting of the imperial consort. This hall is the most magnificent structure in the Grand-View Garden.

沁芳亭桥　为三巷石桥,桥上建亭。据书中描述,"沁芳"二字为小说的男主人公贾宝玉所题。亭桥建于园内中轴线,四通八达,为诸小径咽喉要路,登亭四顾,园中景色尽收眼底。大观园的许多故事都发生在这里。

Fragrance-Seeping Pavilion Bridge The three-section bridge has a pavilion on it. The name of the bridge was given by Jia Baoyu, the main character of the novel. All paths in the garden lead to the bridge. From the bridge one has a whole view of the garden. Many stories told in the novel took place around the bridge.

"怡红快绿" 是宝玉的卧室。院内甬路相衔，山石点缀，蕉棠滴翠，蔷薇吐艳；正殿五门抱厦，绿窗朱门。整个院落富丽堂皇，雍容华贵。这里是金陵十二钗经常聚会，频繁活动的中心。

"Happy Red and Delightful Green" It is the bedroom of Jia Baoyu. The courtyard is decorated with rockeries and crabberry trees. The main house has green screens and crimson pillars. It was the main gathering place of the 12 beauties in the novel.

怡红院 为贾宝玉的住所，三间垂花门楼，四面抄手游廊，粉墙环护，绿柳周垂，房屋豪华气派，以示房主是达官豪门之后。

Happy Red Courtyard It was the living quarter of Jia Baoyu. The main house has three rooms. Corridors go around the wall in pink color. Willow trees give a tranquil atmosphere.

卧室内景　着红袍者为宝玉。他虽出身显贵，却鄙视功名富贵，厌恶趋炎附势，其言行不合时宜，处处表现出他背叛封建家庭的叛逆性格。正因为如此，他与林黛玉的真挚爱情遭到无情打击和摧残，终使他落发为僧。

Inside the bedroom of Jiao Baoyu The statue in red robe is of Jiao Baoyu, the main character in the novel. He despised official-dom and wealth against his family's tradi-tion. The love between him and Lin Daiyu was ruined by his elders. Finally he left home to become a Buddhist monk.

潇湘馆　小说女主人公林黛玉的住所,建筑以淡绿色为主调,屋前翠竹掩映,屋后荷叶田田,环境清静优雅而恬适,借以展示馆中主人寄人篱下、内心悲苦而又孤高自许的心态。

Bamboo Lodge It is the living quarter of Lin Daiyu, the female main character in the novel. The house is dominated by the color of green. In front of the house are bamboo stalks and behind the house there is a patch of field planted with lotus flowers. The environment is quiet but depressing to show the master's feelings as a sad girl living in other's house.

潇湘馆内景　抚琴者为黛玉蜡像。黛玉因父母双亡,长期寄居外祖母家,遂与表兄宝玉相爱。但他们双双蔑视权势利禄,经常流露反抗情绪,不为封建家庭所容。在宝玉被骗与薛宝钗成婚的当晚,她焚稿断诗情,呕血而死。

Inside Bamboo Lodge The wax figure playing a lute is Lin Daiyu. Her parents died and she had to stay with her grandmother on her mother's side. She fell in love with her cousin Jiao Baoyu. Both of them were rebelious against imperial conventions and their love was not approved by their elders. Lin Daiyu died of sadness after learning that Jiao Baoyu had been deceived into marrying Xue Baochai.

衡芜苑　是小说另一主人公薛宝钗的住所。院内怪石嶙峋，异峰突起，仅留一曲径通向正殿前门；这里花草繁茂，青藤缠绕，以展示这位大门闺秀表面温柔敦厚，实则谙于心计的性格特征。

Alpinia Park It is the living quarter of Xue Baochai, another major character in the novel. The courtyard has many rockeries in strange shapes and plants. Only one path leads to the main house. The atmosphere shows the character of its master: externally docile and obedient and internally crafty.

暖香坞　是小说中金陵十二钗之一惜春的住所。因这里比别处暖和，十冬腊月打起腥红毡门帘，仍觉温香拂面，正适合惜春作画，所以叫"暖香坞"。

Smart Weed Breeze Cot It is the living quarter of Jia Xichun, one of the 12 beauties in the novel. Jia Xichun loved painting and liked the room very warm during winter.

藕香榭　　为大观园的点景建筑，正景三间，左右曲廊，竹桥跨水接岸。傍岸植桂，花香四溢，是隔水赏桂的好地方。

Lotus Fragrance Anchorage　The scenic structure has corridors on both sides and is linked with the shore by a bamboo bridge. Sweet osmanthus bushes on the shore emit exquisite aroma when they are in bloom in autumn.

稻香村　是金陵十二钗之一李纨的住处。
这里有竹篱茅亭,果树稻田,水井酒幌;室内
为纸窗木榻,素椅木桌,一洗富贵气象。游
人至此,感觉到的是山村野趣、田园风光。

Paddy-Sweet Cottage It is the living quarter of Li Wan, one of the 12 beauties in the novel. The courtyard is surrounded with bamboo fence. Inside there are a thatched hut, rice paddies and fruit trees. A wine store banner hangs at the gate. The windows are covered with　paper and the tables and chairs are of raw wood.

缀景楼　是金陵十二钗之一迎春的住所。双层楼阁临池而建,池中岸边荇翠菱紫,景色醉人。迎春许配出园后,宝玉天天来这里徘徊瞻顾,只见缀景楼轩窗寂寞,池中菱荷摇摇落落,不胜悲感:池塘一夜秋风冷,吹散菱荷红玉影,蓼花菱叶不胜愁,重露繁霜压纤梗。

Pavilion of Variegated Splendor It is the living quarter of Jia Yingchun, one of the 12 beauties in the novel. The two-story building stands by a pond, in which there are water lilies and water chestnuts. After Yingchun was married, Baoyu often came here and felt sad. In deep autumn when the lotus flowers had withered the scene was even more depressing.

滴翠亭　依照小说中"宝钗戏彩蝶"的故事而建的湖心亭。亭四面为游廊,一座曲桥接岸。登亭可闻水声,可观园景,亦可品茗抒情。

Dripping Emerald Pavilion The pavilion in the lake was where Xue Baochai played with butterflies in the novel. Corridors run around the pavilion and a bridge leads to the bank. People like to come here to hear the sound of flowing water over a cup of tea.

凹晶溪馆　建于园中低洼近水处, 故名
"凹溪", 它与山脊上的凸碧山庄形成对景。
这一上一下, 一高一低, 一山一水专为赏月
而设。

Aojingxi Studio It is located at a low spot
in the garden near water. The structure
and the Tubi Mountain Villa on top of a
hill make a good match. From the two
spots one can have a good view of a bright
moon.

凸碧山庄　因耸立在高峰上而得名。中
秋时节, 贾母率众人在山庄赏月品笛, 甚感
凄清; 黛玉和湘云在溪馆近水赏月, 闻笛联
诗, 尤觉悲凉, 于是引出"寒塘渡鹤影, 冷月
葬花魂"的绝唱, 预示贾府的衰落为期不远。

Tubi Mountain Villa In the middle of autumn, Mother Jai, the matriarch in the novel, led the whole family at this spot to enjoy
the moon the last time before the family
collapsed. Lin Daiyu and Shi Xiangyun
liked to come here to play lute and com-
pose poems.

125

长 城

　　长城是中国古代重要的军事设施。始建于公元前七世纪。秦始皇统一中国后,为防止北方匈奴贵族南下骚扰,于公元前214年开始将各诸侯国建造的长城予以修复、增筑、连接,历时10年,构成庞大的整体。以后历代王朝都根据自己的防御需要,加以重修。到了明代,前后修筑长城18次,历时约200年,使它西起甘肃省的嘉峪关,东至河北省的山海关,越群山,过草地,穿沙漠,横跨6省1市,总长达6700余公里,大部分至今基本完好。

　　北京八达岭长城是明长城的代表。城墙高8.5米,顶宽5.7米,女墙高1米,蜿蜒曲折,气势非凡,实为世界一大奇观。

The Great Wall

长城 据卫星遥感，北京地区共有明代长城 629 公里，以八达岭、慕田峪、金山岭等地段的长城保存最完整。图为八达岭长城鸟瞰。

The Great Wall The Great Wall in the Beijing area is 629 kilometers long. Sections at Badaling, Mutianyu and Jinshanling are the best preserved. The picture shows the section at Badaling.

The Great Wall was a gigantic defence work during ancient China. Seperate walls were built in the 7th century B.C. by small warring states. After the unification of central China, Emperor Qin Shihuang ordered in 214 B.C. to link up those walls in the north to prevent the Huns from coming to the south. The construction continued over 10 years. The Great Wall undertook 18 major repairs and extensions over 200 years during the Ming Dynasty (1368-1644). It runs 6,700 kilometers from Jiayuguan Pass in Gansu Province in the west to Shanhaiguan Pass in Hebei Province in the east over six provinces and Beijing and passes through high mountains, broad grasslands and immense deserts. Most of the Great Wall has remained in good conditions.

The section of the Great Wall at Badaling in Beijing is now a famous tourist attraction. It is 8.5 meters high with breast work of one meter high and 5.7 meters wide at the top.

居庸关 是北京通往蒙古高原的必经之路,关隘建于两山夹峙中,其隘如线,自古为绝险关口。由于这里自然环境优美,远在金代,"居庸叠翠"就是燕京八景之一。

Juyong Pass A point of strategic importance on the road between Beijing and Inner Mongolia, it is located between two sheer mountains. "Piled Emerald at Juyong" was one of the Eight Grand Sights in Beijing during the Liao Dynasty.

云台　为居庸关主要建筑之一，原为寺塔基座，台下为北上通衢，故云台又称过街塔。

Yuntai (Cloud Terrace) One of the main structures at Juyong Pass, it was originally the foundation of a temple pagdoa. A road passes under it from north to south.

云台浮雕　云台券洞内有四大天王和纹饰浮雕，刻工精细，形象生动，是石雕中的精品。

Carvings on Yuntai On the stone wall of the vault at Yuntai there are the portraits of the Four Heavenly Kings, a master piece of relief carving.

八达岭长城　城墙由南北双向倚山而上，南北二峰各有四座敌楼耸立，气势宏伟，景象壮观。

Great Wall at Badaling The section of the Great Wall runs up and down a mountain ridge. Four watch towers rise majestically on top of two peaks to its north and south.

长城瑞雪

Great Wall in winter.

晖映蛟龙

The Great Wall undulates in the mountain like a dragon.

长龙行云

The grace of the Great Wall.

古城夕照

Great Wall at sunset.

134

黄花镇　古为军事重镇,此镇管辖范围包括慕田峪在内的 90 公里长城,是直接护卫明代皇陵的"一级长城",号称"京师北门"。

Huanghua Town In ancient time the town was an army commanding post in charge of a section of the Great Wall of 90 kilometers at Mutianyu. Because it was the nearest part to Beijing it was made First-Class Wall and known as "Northern Gate to the Capital".

慕田峪长城　位于北京东北约 70 公里处。明洪武元年（1368 年），大将徐达筑边墙，自山海关抵慕田峪。此段长城以雄伟险峻著称，加之山势峥嵘，自然环境优美，颇有高山园林的特色。

Great Wall at Mutianyu In 1368 General Xu Da of the Ming Dynasty built the Great Wall from Shanhaiguan to Mutianyu. The part in Mutianyu, 70 kilometers from Beijing City, is well known for its dangerous terrain and beautiful surroundings.

金山岭长城　因建于人、小金山而得名。它位于北京市密云县和河北省滦平县交界处，是古北口长城的东段。古北口长城"南控幽燕，北捍溯漠"，素称"京师锁钥"。金山岭长城以明长城为主体，全长 25 公里。

Great Wall at Jinshanling The section of the Great Wall at Jinshanling runs on top of Greater and Minor Jinshan Mountains along the border between Miyun County of Beijing and Luanxian County of Hebei Province. It is the eastern part of the Great Wall of Gubeikou, a strategic point safeguarding the capital. The whole section is 25 kilometers long.

敌楼　　此段长城共设敌楼140座,且造型多样,有台形、扁形、圆形,还有船篷顶、平顶、穹隆顶,应有尽有。敌楼一般分上下两层,纵横6条拱道,10个券门,也有三层的大楼。每座敌楼都有名称,诸如姐妹楼、黑楼、花楼、将军楼、仙女楼、望京楼,如此等等。

Watch towers There are 140 watch towers on the Great Wall in the Jinshanling section. They are of various shapes: some are platforms, some are circular; some have a roof like a boat and some have a flat roof. A watch tower is usually of two stories and has six tunnels and 10 openings. Some larger ones have three floors. All of them have names such as Sisters Tower, Black Tower, Flower Tower, Fairy Maid Tower and Looking Toward the Capital Tower.

司马台关城　为明代所建,原关口已淹沉水中。此关西南不远处即是烟波浩渺的密云水库。这里峰峦迭嶂,长城起伏,波光照影,风景迷人。图为司马台关城——二龙戏珠。

Simatai Fort Built during the Ming Dynasty, the fort had submerged in water long time ago. Not far from it is the immense Miyun Reservoir. The Great Wall undulates gracefully among high mountain peaks. The picture shows the "Two Dragons Playing with a Pearl" at Simatai.

明十三陵

明十三陵位于北京西北郊约 50 公里处。陵区以长陵所在的天寿山为主峰,东、西、北三面群山环抱,构成一座天然大庭院,院门南开,蟒山、虎山雄峙两侧,似一龙一虎镇守大门。向南是宽阔的盆地,温榆河从西北蜿蜒流来。明代自成祖朱棣至思宗朱由检等 13 位皇帝就埋在这群山环绕、松柏掩映的区域内,总面积约 40 多平方公里。

明十三陵从永乐 7 年(1409 年)始建长陵起,至崇祯 17 年(1644 年)修建思陵止,历时 200 余年,其工程之大,耗时之长,在中国陵墓营建史上绝无仅有。当初,整个陵区方圆数十公里内为一片禁区,曾蒙上许多神秘色彩。

1956 年,中国文物考古工作者发掘了明万历皇帝朱翊钧的陵墓——定陵,发现了地下宫殿,除棺椁外,出土金银珠宝、服饰玉器等宝物 3000 多件,揭开了定陵的秘密。1959 年 10 月建立了定陵博物馆。从此,明十三陵成为北京地区著名的旅游胜地。

The Ming Tombs

石牌坊　十三陵的第一座建筑物，建于嘉靖 19 年(1540 年)，为 5 间 6 柱 11 顶全石结构，夹柱石四面雕龙，座顶为麒麟，牌坊整体造型宏伟。

Stone Archway The first structure a visitor sees at the Ming Tombs is a stone archway. Built in 1540, it has five sections, six pillars and 11 roofs. The square pillars bear carvings of dragons on the sides and a unicorn on the top.

The Ming Tombs are located 50 kilometers to the northwest of downtown Beijing. The burial ground of 13 emperors of the Ming Dynasty (1368-1644) is embraced by mountains on three sides and opening to a flat basin on the south. Mangshan and Hushan mountains rise on either side. The Wenyu River flows to the northwest. The whole area of 40 square kilometers is covered with ancient pine and cypress trees.

Changling, the oldest mausoleum in the center of the burial complex on Tianshou Mountain, was built in 1409 and Siling, the last mausoleum of the Ming Tombs, was built in 1644, 200 years after the first one. It was the most costly construction project with the longest time in the construction of imperial burial grounds in China. In those days the area with a circumference of several dozen kilometers was tightly guarded, giving it a myterious atmosphere.

In 1956 Chinese archaeologists excavated Ding ling, the tomb of Emperor Wen Li (Zhu Yijun) and unearthed 3,000 pieces of gold, silver, jade and precious stone except the confins of the emperor and his empresses. A museum was established at the site in October 1959. Since then the Ming Tombs have been a favorite tourist spot.

碑楼　为重檐庑殿式,顶覆黄琉璃瓦。楼内是高 10 多米、龙首龟趺的石碑,碑铭为"长陵神功圣德碑",碑楼四角各立云龙华表一座。

Stele Tower The tower of multiple eaves with yellow glazed tiles keeps a 10-meter-high stone tablet sitting on a stone turtle with a dragon's head. The inscription on the tablet reads: "Divine merits and holy virtues of Dingling". Four stone pillars carved with dragons and clouds stand on the four corners of the tower.

神路　蜿蜒曲折长约 10 公里,道两边分列着 18 对石人石兽。其中石人 12 座,分别为勋臣、文臣和武将,均为站像;石兽为 24 座,它们是豸(传说中的怪兽)、骆驼、象、麒麟和马,姿态各异,或立或卧,蔚为壮观。

Divine Path Flanking the 10-kilometer-long path are 18 pairs of stone sculptures of human figures and animals. The 12 standing human figures represent civil and military court officials and the 24 animals are *xie* (a mysterious animal in Chinese mythology), camels, elephants, *qilin* (another animal in Chinese mythology) and horses.

长陵全景　　长陵是十三陵的首陵，从破土至完工用了 5 年，里面埋葬的是明代第三帝朱棣。明代各陵统称"宫"，原有宫墙围括。长陵宫门内分别为祾恩门、祾恩殿、明楼和宝城，另有祠祭署、神宫监、神厨、神库、宰牲亭等附属建筑，整座陵宫是一座庞大的建筑群。

Changling The oldest tomb of the 13 Ming Tombs was built in five years for Zhu Li, the third emperor of the Ming Dynasty. Originally there was a wall around the mount with a gate. The Ling'en Hall, Ming Tower, Precious City and some auxiliary establishments for sacrificial rituals and storage have remained.

长陵祾恩殿　是帝、后或遗官祭陵行礼的大殿,建在 3 层白石台基上,重檐垂脊,面宽 9 间,深 5 间,全木结构,是中国现存最大的木构架建筑。

Ling'en Hall of Changling The main structure of the mausoleum was used by the living emperor and his empress to pay respect to the dead emperor buried in Changling. It stands on a three-tier white marble terrace and has sloping roof with multiple eaves. This hall is the largest wooden structure still in existence from ancient times in China.

裬恩殿内景　走进大殿,楠木的芳香扑鼻而来,殿内 60 根楠木大柱均采自中国西南深山,一根巨木从采伐到运出林区,需数年,许多民工为此丧命。

Inside the Ling'en Hall The hall is permeated with the scent from the 60 nanmu pillars. A nanmu tree needed several years and cost many lives to be transported to Beijing from forests deep in the mountains in southwest China.

定陵全景　定陵建在长陵西南的大峪山下,是十二陵中的第 10 座陵,埋葬着明代第 13 帝朱翊钧和他的两位皇后。

A whole view of Dingling Dingling at the foot of Dayu Mountain southwest of Changling is the 10th tomb of the Ming Tombs for Zhu Yijun, the 13th emperor of the Ming Dynasty and his two empresses.

定陵明楼　高 21.32 米，座落于方城之上，重檐歇山顶，其椽坊、斗拱均为白石凿成，再施彩绘，坚实美观。楼内立石碑，碑额篆"大明"二字，碑身刻"神宗显皇帝之陵"七字。明楼是各陵的标志。

Ming Tower of Dingling The 21.32 meter-high tower on the wall has a gabled roof with multiple eaves. The beams and brackets are made of white marble and painted with colors. The two characters on the top of a stone tablet inside the tower read "Daming (Great Ming)" and the several characters on the front side read: "In Memory of Emperor of Divinity and Eminence".

定陵宝城　是一道圆形的砖围墙,设有垛口,周长约750米,围墙内封土下即是墓室。

Precious City of Dingling It is a round enclosure of a brick wall of 750 meters. Under the earth mount inside the enclosure is the burial chamber.

地宫入口　地宫共有7道石门,为整块汉白玉石雕成,前、中、后3道门最大,高3.3米,宽1.8米,重约4吨,门正面有9排共81枚乳状门钉和铺首(门环底座)。石门制作工整,安装紧密。

Entrance to the Underground Palace There are seven entrances to the burial chamber underground. Each was blocked by a large piece of white marble. Those blocks of the front, middle and back entrances are the largest: 3.3 meters high, 1.8 meters wide and weighing four tons. On the front side of each stone slab there are 81 knobs in nine rows. The stone door pannels are meticulously carved and closely fitted to the entrance.

甬道　是地宫通往各殿的走道。地宫是陵
的主要部分，为全石拱券式无梁建筑，全长
87.34 米, 宽 47.28 米, 由 5 个殿组成, 总面
积 1195 平方米。

Tunnels They lead to the burial chamber, called underground palace. The underground vault, entirely built with stone slabs without beams and pillars, is 87.34 meters long and 47.28 meters wide, comprises five halls and has an area of 1,195 square meters.

长明灯　安置在中殿,共3尊,青花云龙纹大瓷缸内装香油,地宫封闭时长明灯尚亮,后因缺氧自灭。

Everlasting Lamps Three large porcelain jars in the center of the central hall were filled with sesame oil. They were supposed to keep the light on forever. But the lack of oxygen after the vault was closed put the lamps out.

棺椁　置于地宫玄殿（后殿）。殿高 9.5 米，长 30.1 米，宽 9.1 米。棺床上存放皇帝朱翊钧和孝端、孝靖两皇后的棺椁，皇帝居中，皇后分列左右。棺椁两边摆放 26 只装有陪葬品的朱漆木箱。棺椁周围还有玉器、青花瓷瓶等物。

Confins The confins are placed in the rear hall. The rear hall is 9.5 meters high, 30.1 meters long and 9.1 meters wide. The confins for Emperor Zhu Yijun and Empresses Xiao Tuan and Xiao Jing are placed on a platform. Twenty-six lacquered boxes on either side of the confins contain sacrificial objects. Jade and porcelain objects are placed around the cofins.

金冠　又名翼善冠，全部用金丝编织而成，孔眼匀称，外表光滑，冠顶二龙戏珠，生动逼真，工艺极为精湛。中国仅此一件，实为国宝。

Gold Crown It is woven with gold thread with close meshes and a smooth surface. The ornament on the top is of two dragons playing with a pearl. This is the only imperial gold crown in China.

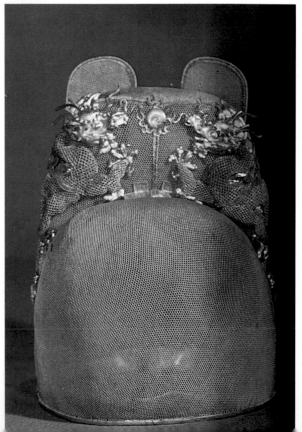

凤冠　为皇后朝会大典时戴。冠上饰有花丝金龙、翠凤和珠宝镶装的花卉，共用珍珠 5000 余颗，宝石 150 余块，造型雍容富丽，华贵异常。

Pheonix Crown The empress wore the pheonix crown at grand ceremonies. It is decorated with a dragon woven with gold thread, a pheonix made of emerald and flowers made of precious stones. A total of 5,000 pearls and 150 pieces of precious stones were used.

永陵　建于陵区阳翠岭下，为明代皇帝朱厚熜之陵，原建规模甚大，为诸陵之首。从现存明楼可以看出其额枋、斗拱全部为石结构，楼上涂彩绘，地上铺文石，这种石料滑润如脂，坚硬似钢；楼上竖石碑，上刻"大明世宗肃皇帝之陵"。永陵除明楼和宝城外，其他建筑基本无存。

Yongling The tomb at the foot of Yangcui Mountain is for Emperor Shi Zong (Zhu Houcong). It was the largest of the Ming Tombs when it was built. Beams and brackets of the Ming Tower are all of stone. The tower is painted with color and the ground is paved with veined stones which are known for their hardness and smoothness. The front side of a stone tablet in the Ming Tower bears the inscription: "In memory of Emperor Shi Zong of the Great Ming". Only the Ming Tower and Precious City have been left.

景陵　为宣德皇帝朱瞻基之陵。景陵和献陵在诸陵中较简陋，规模亦小。

Jingling It is the tomb for Emperor Xuan De (Zhu Zhanji). Jingling and Xianling are the simplest and smallest tombs of the 13 Ming Tombs.

雍和宫

雍和宫是北京最大的喇嘛庙。位于城区东北安定门内。它建于清康熙33年(1694年),原为清雍正皇帝即位前的府邸,称雍亲王府;雍正即位后将王府一半改为黄教上院,一半作为皇家游乐园。雍正3年(1725年)改为今名。雍正皇帝驾崩后因在此停放灵枢,故将宫内永佑殿、法轮殿等主要殿堂改易黄瓦,大部分殿宇为喇嘛诵经之所。

雍和宫由牌楼院、昭泰门、天王殿、雍和宫、永佑殿、法轮殿、万福阁等7进院落组成。各院落及其建筑,无一雷同。院落由南至北渐次缩小,而建筑物则渐次升高,这种"正殿高大而重院深藏"、"宫门向阳而层层掩护"的建筑格局,颇有聚龙窝凤的庄严气象。这正是中国传统的古建风格的完美体现。整个建筑巍峨壮丽,并兼有汉、满、蒙、藏民族特色。

雍和宫各殿供有众多佛像,还藏有大量珍贵文物,其中五百罗汉山、金丝楠木佛龛和18米高的白檀木大佛最负盛名,被称为雍和宫的木雕三绝。

Yonghegong Lamasery

鸟瞰雍和宫　众多殿堂楼阁、宝枋、角亭构成一组规模宏大的建筑群。它是北京保护最完整的喇嘛庙。

A bird's-eye view of Yonghegong Lamasery The many halls, towers, archways and corner towers form a majestic complex of buildings. It is the best preserved temple of Tibetan Buddhism in Beijing.

The largest temple of Tibetan Buddhism is located near Andingmen city gate in northeastern Beijing. It was built in 1694 as the residence of Emperor Yong Zheng when he was crown prince. After he moved into the imperial palace the new emperor turned half of his former residence into a lamaist temple of the Yellow Sect and the other half into a garden. The present name was given in 1725. The Hall of Yongyou and Hall of Wheel of the Law and some other main structures were reroofed with yellow glazed tiles when the dead Emperor Yong Zheng lay in state in the temple.

The whole ground of the temple is composed of seven courtyards divided by an Archway Compound, Zhaotai Gate, Hall of Heavenly Kings, Yonghe Palace, Yongyou Hall, Hall of Wheel of the Law and Wanfu Tower. The courtyards become smaller from north to south while the buildings become higher, a perfect combination of central China, Manchu, Mongol and Tibetan architectural styles.

The lamasery keeps a great number of Buddhist statues and cultural relics. A jade carving of 500 arhats, nanmu wood niche with gold thread and a 18-meter-high statue of Buddha are the best known treasures in the temple.

牌楼　又称宝坊。位于雍和宫正南,由 3
座牌楼组成一牌楼院。1939 年 8 月,侵占
北京的日本军队用水泥梁柱偷换了牌楼的
金丝楠木梁柱,并将主要构件运回日本。图
为被偷梁换柱的牌楼。

Archways The three archways in front of
the southern gate were originally made of
gold-veined nanmu wood. In August 1939
Japanese soldiers took the wooden pillars
to Japan and replaced them with cement.

The Hall of Heavenly Kings (Yonghe Gate) The name plaque above the entrance to the hall,
the first main hall and the front entrance to the temple, is in four languages of Han, Manchu,
Mongolian and Tibetan.

天王殿(雍和门)　为雍和宫的第一进大殿。这是一座明五暗十的殿堂,殿前檐正中悬挂乾隆皇帝
用汉、满、蒙、藏 4 种文字亲题的"雍和门"匾额。此殿原为雍亲王府的正门,改成喇嘛庙后为庙的山门。

布袋尊者　端坐于天王殿正中金漆雕龙宝座上,坦胸露乳,笑容可掬。中国民间称他大肚弥勒佛。他原名契此,五代时后梁(公元 907－923 年)人,居浙江奉化。传说他手挽布袋,见物即乞,但将所得悉数捐赠寺院,自称是未来佛弥勒佛转世。

Sage of Cloth Bag Popularly known as Potted Belly Maitreya, the Buddha's secular name was Qici, a native of Fenghua in Zhejiang Province who lived during the Five Dynasties period (907-923). A story tells that he begged with a cloth bag and denoted all he got to Buddhist temples. He called himself reincarnation of the Future Buddha.

韦驮　面北立于天王殿后门。据传,他是释迦牟尼舍利子塔的护卫者。举凡寺庙,他总立于第一进大殿的后门,作为庙宇的护法神。

Weituo The divine gardian of the Pagoda of Sakyamuni's Relics stands at the back door of the Hall of Heavenly Kings. The statue is found at the back door of the main hall in every Buddhist temple.

铜鼎 立于雍和宫大殿前,1747 年铸造,高 4 米,6 个火焰喷门,通体有精美浮雕,鼎足为 3 个形如雄狮的狻猊头像,造型古朴浑厚、持重稳健。中国现存仅两座。

Bronze burner The bronze burner in front of the main hall of the temple was cast in 1747. It is four meters high and has six openings to release smoke. Its well polished wall bears elaborately carved designs. Its three feet are in the shape of a lion. China has only two such bronze burners.

雍和宫 为面阔 7 间、前出廊后带厦的大殿,原是雍亲王接见文武官员的地方,改为喇嘛庙后相当于庙的大雄宝殿,内供 3 尊铜质三世佛像。

Yonghe Palace Originally it was the place Prince Yong received officials. When the prince's mansion became a temple it was renovated to be the Daxiong Hall. Inside the hall there are bronze statues of Trikala Buddhas.

三世佛　正中是现在佛释迦牟尼佛，其东
为未来佛弥勒佛，西为过去佛燃灯佛。

Trikala Buddhas In the middle is Sakyamuni and on either side are the Future
Buddha and Past Buddha.

十八罗汉　　相传是释迦牟尼的 18 位弟子,受佛旨意常留人间,宣扬佛法。当年塑造这些罗汉时,罗汉全身包金,金上涂染料,待其干后再用刻刀把需要露出部位的染料轻轻剔除,使精美的花纹和图饰环绕罗汉全身,这就是中国独有的"拨金术"。这些罗汉历经 300 余年,至今光彩照人,图纹生动细腻,为中国雕塑艺术品中的佳作。

18 Arhats The 18 arhats were disciples of Sakyamuni. On his death, the Great Buddha ordered them to stay in the secular world to propagate the Law. The statues were made by wrapping the base with gold foil, painting the gold layer with colors and then scuplting on the paint to reveal beautiful designs. After 300 years the statues still as bright as new.

四面护法　供于雍和宫东翼楼,为四首四臂,面目狰狞,因其专司护法,故名四面护法神。

Four-Direction Gardian of the Law The divine gardian of the Law in a wing tower on the eastern side of the temple has four heads and four arms and a horrifying expression.

永佑殿　原为雍亲王的寝殿,雍正帝死后曾停灵柩于此,名永佑殿,似有永保雍正帝亡灵之意。

Yongyou Hall It was originally the bedroom of Prince Yong. After he died as Emperor Yong Zheng his confine was kept in this hall.

永佑殿内景　三尊高 2.35 米的佛像,均为白檀木精雕而成。居中一尊头戴五佛冠、手托宝瓶的是无量寿佛,左为药师佛,右为狮吼佛。

Inside the Yongyou Hall The three 2.35-meter-high statues of Buddha were carved out of a whole piece of white sandalwood. The one in the middle with a Five-Buddha crown and a precious bottle is Aparimitayus. On his left is Bhaisajya-guruvaiduryaprabhasa and on his right is Shihou Buddha.

法轮殿　面宽 7 间,前后各出抱厦 5 间,平面呈"十"字形。楼顶仿西藏寺院建 5 座铜质镏金宝塔,塔檐悬若干风铃,风吹铃响,气氛肃穆。这里是众喇嘛讲经说法、举行佛事活动的场所。

The Hall of Wheel of the Law The seven-bay wide and five-bay deep hall sits on a cross-shaped foundation. The roof is topped with five gilt copper balls with a number of small copper bells hanging from the eaves. It is where lamas chant prayers.

Lamas chanting prayer The 6.1-meter-high copper statue in the center of the Hall of the Wheel of the Law is of Tsongkhapa, founder of the Buddhist Yellow Sect. Tsongkhapa was a native of Huangzhong County in Qinghai Province and studied Lamaism in Tibet. He was profoundly disturbed by corrupted Buddhist monks of the Mi Sect and was determined to carry out reforms. He won popular support and founded a new sect: the Yellow Sect. Followers of this sect wear yellow hats and robes.

众喇嘛在法轮殿做佛事　　正中供的是高 6.1 米的宗喀巴大师铜像。宗喀巴出生于青海湟中县，曾赴西藏研究喇嘛教学说，他对该教只重密宗，不习显宗，崇尚咒语，不重戒律颇不安，尤其对某些教徒生活腐化深感痛心，立志革除弊端，他被拥戴为领袖，由于他的努力，逐步形成新的教派 —— 格鲁派。此派戴黄帽、穿黄衣，所以又称黄教。

法轮殿壁画　描绘于殿内东西山墙上，名为《释迦牟尼源流图》，共 34 段，详绘了佛祖从降生、学艺、出家、成佛和传教的过程。

Muruals in the Hall of the Wheel of the Law The 34 sections of wall painting in the hall depict Sakyamuni of his birth, study, becoming a monk and finally the Buddha in detail.

164

五百罗汉山　珍藏于法轮殿,山体用檀香木精雕而成,五百罗汉用金、银、铜、铁、锡5种金属制成,是一组艺术珍品。

500-Arhat Mount The carving is made of sandalwood while the 500 arhats of gold, silver, copper, iron and zinc.

万福阁 为全木结构,阁高 25 米,飞檐 3 重,斗拱交构,壮丽异常。万福阁东西并肩排列着重檐楼阁两座,西为延绥阁,东为永康阁,二楼以飞廊与万福阁连为一体,峥嵘崔巍,犹如琼楼玉宇、仙阁神宫。

Wanfu Tower The wooden tower with mutiple eaves is 25 meters high. Standing on either side of it are the Yansui Tower to the west and Yongkang Tower to the east. The two side towers are connected with the Wanfu Tower by corridors.

旃檀佛 供于万福阁的东翼楼,为仿木铜铸佛像,其水纹衣饰、哈达均为铜质,却给人以柔软飘逸之感。佛龛和火焰背光系金丝楠木制成,共雕有 99 条蟠龙,大有群龙腾舞、呼之欲出的感觉。

Tongtan Buddha The statue in the eastern wing tower by the Wanfu Tower is made of copper in imitation of wood. The ornaments on the clothes and silk *hada* ribbons are also of copper but appear like real material. A niche and the flaming aura behind the Buddha's head are made of gold-veined nanmu wood. The 99 dragons look like to come out any time.

迈达拉佛　佛名为蒙语，汉语即未来佛。佛高 18 米，地下还有 8 米，是用整棵白檀木雕凿而成的。游人至此若看佛面，颇有仰目落冠之势。

Maidala Buddha Maidala means Future Buddha in Mongolian language. The statue is 18 meters high, with eight meters underground. It is carved out of a whole piece of white sandalwood.

大钟寺（觉生寺）

大钟寺座落于北京北三环西路。

清代雍正年间（公元 1723 - 1736 年），皇帝到北京西郊游览，认为此地"右隔城市之嚣，左绕山川之胜，宜寂静清修之地，用是肇建梵宇"。遂于雍正 11 年（1733 年）建寺，是年正月开工，次年冬月告竣，赐名觉生寺。后因永乐大钟从万寿寺移此，故俗称大钟寺，而雍正皇帝钦定的正名却鲜为人知。

寺坐北朝南，布局严谨对称，自南而北的中轴线上依次为影壁（已毁）、山门、天王殿、大雄宝殿、观音殿、藏经楼和大钟楼等，其两侧分别为钟鼓楼、东西配殿和群房。大钟寺历经 260 年的风风雨雨，各殿佛像早已无存，惟永乐大钟仍悬挂于大钟楼。

1957 年大钟寺被列为北京市重点文物保护单位，1985 年辟为"大钟寺古钟博物馆"，内藏各类古钟数百件，同时恢复了传统的春节庙会。大钟寺从此以新的面貌接待中外游客。

Juesheng Temple

大钟寺山门 山门上方石刻匾额"敕建觉生寺"为雍正皇帝御笔。山门朱墙灰顶，古朴庄重，门内各殿亦为灰顶歇山式建筑，其建筑规格虽然平平，但在古文献《京师二百九十一座寺庙细数析》中，因永乐大钟闻名，它的名次排列第三。

Front gate of the temple The name of the temple on the front gate is in the handwriting of Emperor Yong Zheng. The wall is painted crimson and the roof is covered with grey tiles. The buildings inside the gate also have gray roofs. Although the temple does not look very elegant, but it was placed as the third holiest temple of the 291 temples in the Beijing area by a history book.

The Juesheng Temple, commonly known as Dazhong (Giant Bell) Temple, is located on the western part of the Third Ring Road north of downtown Beijing. Emperor Yong Zheng who reigned between 1723 and 1736 described the area as "being seperated from noises and ideal for a temple." So a Buddhist temple was built there in 1733 and named Juesheng. A giant bell cast during the Yongle period was moved from the Wanshou Temple to the Juesheng Temple later.

The layout of the temple is neat and compact. From south to north along a central axis are a screen wall (destroyed), the front gate, Hall of Heavenly Kings, Daxiong Hall, Guanyin Hall, Scripture Tower and Giant Bell Tower. On either side of them are bell and drum towers, wing halls and houses. Buddhst statues in the temple have been lost during its history of 260 years. Only the giant bell still hangs in the Giant Bell Tower.

The temple was listed as a key site under national protection in 1957 and in 1985 it became the Dazhongsi Museum of Ancient Bells. Several hundred bells are on display. On every Spring Festival a traditional fair with various amusement events is held.

大雄宝殿　原为供奉释迦牟尼佛像的殿堂,现为古钟第一陈列室。

Daxiong Hall It used to have a statue of Sakyamuni but now is the first exhibition room of the museum of ancient bells.

大雄宝殿内景　内存 1978 年出土的战国(前 475－前 221 年)曾侯乙编钟。这些编钟演奏乐曲时音域宽广,音色浑厚圆润,富有较强的表现力,显示中国古编钟发展至战国时工艺已趋完美。

Inside the Daxiong Hall The hall today keeps a set of musical bells excavated in 1978. They belonged to a marquis Zenghouyi who lived in the **Warring** States Period (475-221 B.C.) The sound of the bells has a broad range and is very expressive.

东群房钟林　大钟寺内陈列的古钟,远至原始社会陶钟,近至民国道钟,有大有小,大者二层楼高,小者如同酒盅。漫步钟林,宛若在历史长河中揽胜。

Bell Forest The houses on the eastern part of the temple display a big array of bells from pottery bells of the premitive society to bells made during modern times. The largest bell is as high as a two-story building and the smallest bell is of the size of a wine cup.

乾隆朝钟 造型极为美观,钟壁蛟龙栩栩如生。钟体未铸款识,仅在钟唇上铸有 8 个"☰",这是八卦中的"乾卦",加上钟壁上的蛟龙(汉语"龙""隆"谐音),暗款为乾隆年间铸造。

Court Bell of Qian Long The beautiful bell cast during the reign of Emperor Qian Long bears carvings of dragons on its wall. There are no inscriptions but only eight sets of "☰", a symbol of the Eight Diagrams.

钟楼　为大钟寺最具特色的核心建筑，耸立在巨大的青石台基上。楼形上圆下方，象征"天圆地方"。楼内悬挂着永乐大钟。

Bell Tower The central building of the temple stands on a gray stone foundation. The tower is round at the lower part and square at the upper part, symbolizing the ancient belief that "Heaven is round and earth is square." A giant bell cast during the reign of Emperor Yong Le hangs from the ceiling at the center.

永乐大钟　通高 6.75 米，最大直径 3.3 米，重达 46.5 吨，堪称中国钟林之王。

Yongle Bell The bell is 6.75 meters high and 3.3 meters in diameter at the widest section and weighs 46.5 tons. It is called the "King of Bells" in China.

大钟铭文　钟体内外铸有汉文经咒 16 种，梵文咒语 100 余种，共 23 万多字。字体婉丽典雅，笔划工整隽秀，是明代初期馆阁体书法艺术的代表作。

Inscriptions on the Giant Bell Inscribed on the wall of the giant bell are 16 scriptures in Chinese language and 100 scriptures in Sankrit language, with a total number of 230,000 characters. They are representative works of calligraphy from the early Ming Dynasty (1368-1644).

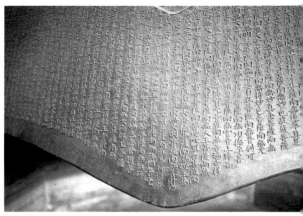

大钟铜销　如此大钟悬挂于梁上，用的竟是一根高 14 厘米、宽 6.5 厘米、长 1 米的铜穿钉。力学专家们测定，它的承受力在安全系数内，原来匠师们在铜销中心铸入了一根相当低碳钢的芯子，以此确保大钟安然无恙。

Copper pin of the Giant Bell The giant bell hangs onto a beam with a copper pin of only 14 centimeters high, 6.5 centimeters wide and one meter long. Mechanics experts found out how a slender pin could bear such a heavy object: a low carbon core was inserted in the copper pin when it was cast.

卢沟桥

卢沟桥位于北京西南郊,因横跨卢沟而得名。卢沟桥一带,是燕地通往华北平原的要津,重要的古渡口。

卢沟桥建于 12 世纪末,工程宏伟,艺术精湛。桥为石砌连续圆拱,整个桥体为石结构,桥墩、拱券等关键部位,嵌有带棱角的铁锭榫,把石间紧紧相连。此外,桥墩平面呈船形,迎水面设分水尖,形似船头,分水尖上还安置了一根边长约 26 厘米的三角铁柱,以减少洪水和冰块的冲击;桥墩顺水面做成流线形,并向内收进如船尾,洪水一出券洞即被分散,大大减弱了洞内水流压力。其次,每一桥墩都肩挑两拱,拱拱相连,构成整体,共同承受负重。据有关部门测试,直到现在,桥的负重仍可达 439 吨,这在世界建桥史上实属罕见。

二次世界大战时,在卢沟桥爆发了震惊中外的"卢沟桥事变",揭开了中国人民抗击侵略者的伟大斗争,卢沟桥从此被载入史册。

Lugou (Marco Polo) Bridge

俯瞰卢沟桥　卢沟之名始于唐代,因河水混浊,又称小黄河,还因河道累迁,亦称无定河。康熙年间(公元1662－1723年)筑长堤防水,于是改名永定河,沿用至今。卢沟桥横架于永定河东西两岸,已历800个春秋,但依然气势雄伟,坚固如初。

A bird's-eye view of Lugou Bridge The name came into being during the Tang Dynasty (618-907). It was also called the Minor Yellow River for its water was very muddy and Wuding (Uncertain) River for it often changed its course. During the reign of Emperor Kang Xi (1662-1723) dykes were built and the name was changed to Yongding (Eternal Stability). The bridge on the river was built 800 years ago.

Lugou (Marco Polo) Bridge crosses the Lugou River in the southwestern outskirts of Beijing. In ancient times the bridge was a key point on the road from Beijing to other parts of North China Plains.

The bridge was built toward the end of the 12th century. The arches are closely arranged and seams at key points are reinforced with cast iron blocks. The piers are in the shape of a boat. An iron triangle is anchored on the boat head to meet the currents. The force of the currents is reduced as the boat-shaped pier spreads it to either side. The closely placed arches are also an important factor to reduce the force of currents. The bridge can still bear a load of 439 tons at a time, a marvelous deed in the world history of bridge building.

In 1938 Japanese provoked an armed incident at Luguo Bridge, launching the war against the Japanese invaders in China.

卢沟桥夕照　桥全长266.5米,桥面宽7.5米,是中国北方最长的古石拱桥。桥面石板久经碾磨,在夕阳照射下,更显凹凸不平,似在向世人倾诉它饱经沧桑的历史。

Sunset at Lugou The bridge is 266.5 meters long and eight meters wide, the longest stone bridge in North China. The stone slabs on the bridge have been well polished over the years and appear still more uneven in the glow of sunset.

桥券洞　桥为石砌连续圆拱桥，共有券洞
11孔，券洞基础牢固，从建桥之初至今，累
经洪水和冰块冲击，仍保持原样，堪称奇迹。

Arches of the bridge There are 11 arches
under the bridge. They have remained intact after a so long time washed by floods
and ice.

石狮　桥上共有望柱 281 根,柱顶均雕有姿态各异的大石狮,另有若干小狮分散在大石狮的身前、背后和爪下,经有关部门清点、编号,共有石狮 496 只。

Stone lions On top of each of the 281 stone balusters on the bridge is the carving of a big lion. On the front, on the back and under the paw of the big lion are smaller lions. A count was made several years ago to put the number at 496.

"卢沟晓月"碑　碑为四柱式宝盖顶,碑高 4.52 米,宽 1.27 米,两侧及四边刻有二龙戏珠浮图,造型别致,雕刻精美,此种碑形在北京尚属首例。碑刻"卢沟晓月"四字为乾隆皇帝御笔。

Stone Stele of "Morning Moon at Lugou" The stele under a stone crown supported with four stone pillars is 4.52 meters high and 1.27 meters wide. On the four sides are carvings in relief of two dragons playing with a pearl. The four characters meaning "Morning Moon at Lugou" are in the handwriting of Emperor Qian Long.

香山公园

香山公园位于北京西山东麓,距城区约 40 公里。西山左拥太行,右揽京城,面对平川,远看颇似一张满弦之弓。18 世纪中叶,清代皇室耗巨资在这里设 28 景,建成香山皇家园林——静宜园,园内殿宇台榭,亭阁塔坊应有尽有,是皇帝避署消夏的离宫。但是,这座规模宏丽的静宜园于 1860 年和 1900 年先后遭英法联军和八国联军两次焚烧,所剩名胜古迹大多残缺不全。新中国成立后,陆续恢复了部分景点,使香山风景区又焕发了生机。公园内以见心斋、双清别墅、昭庙以及与公园为邻的碧云寺和卧佛寺最负盛名。

香山公园是一座典型的森林公园,这里古木扶疏,园林清幽,景色迷人。特别在深秋时节,遍山的黄栌树呈现出"霜叶红于二月花"的动人景象。西山赏秋观红叶成为北京人一年一度的盛会。

Xiangshan (Fragrant Hill) Park

香山公园　园内西南山坡遍植黄栌树,总数近 10 万株,每至深秋,黄栌树叶红似火,艳如霞,把香山装点得绚丽多彩。

Xiangshan Park More than 100,000 smoke trees grow on the southwestern slopes. Around November their leaves turn ruby red to present a magnificent scene.

Frangrant Hill lies on the eastern end of the Western Mountains, 40 kilometers west to Beijing proper. The Western Mountains, a part of the Taihang Mountains, resemble a bow embracing Beijing on the plain. In the mid-18th century, the imperial court of the Qing Dynasty spent a great amount of money on the construction of a grand summer resort on Fragrant Hill -- the Qingyi Garden. In 1860 English and French allied army and in 1890 the army of the Eight-Power Allied Forces invaded Beijing, looting and setting fire on all the famous imperial gardens in the the capital. The palatial halls, towers and pavilions in Qingyi Garden were not spared. After the founding of the People's Repulic in 1949, some of the scenic spots in the garden have been restored. Most famous attractions in Xiangshan Park today are Jianxing (Seeing the Heart) Studio, Shuangqing (Double Clear-Fountain) Villa and Zhao Monastery in the park and Biyun (Azure Cloud) Temple and Wuofo (Sleeping Buddha) Temple near the park.

Fragrant Hill is covered with ancient trees. In late fall the leaves of smoke trees turn ruby red. To admire the red leaves on Fragrant Hill is a favorite item for an outing of Beijing residents.

见心斋　始建于明嘉靖元年(1522 年)，是一处富有江南园林风格的庭院。院内池水清冽，小桥玲珑，回廊曲折，轩榭精巧，是游人理想的憩息之所。

Jianxin Studio Built in 1522 during the Ming Dynasty, the place is an imitation of a small garden south of the Yangtze River. A pond with clear water, an exquisite bridge and corridor provide a good spot for rest.

昭庙　全称"宗镜大昭之庙",是清乾隆皇帝为接待班禅六世而建的。庙的大部分建筑毁于 1860 年。图为已恢复的主体建筑——红台。

Zhao Monastery Emperor Qian Long of the Qing Dynasty built this temple to receive the 6th Penchan Lama who came to visit Beijing from Tibet. Most of the structures in the temple were destroyed in 1860. This Red Terrace is a recent reconstruction.

双清别墅　是融山、泉、树、石、竹为一体的别致小院,院西两股清泉常流不息,泉上崖石间"双清"二字为乾隆皇帝御笔。

Shuangqing Villa The exquisite compound is complete with hills, springs, trees, rockeries and bamboo. Two fountains in the western part gave its name Shuangqing (Double Fountains). The name plaque is in the handwriting of Emperor Qian Long.

香炉峰 为香山主峰,海拔550米,峰上有两块巨石,名乳峰石,立于石上纵目四望,云雾茫茫,树海苍苍,气势磅礴,景象万千。

Xianglu (Incense Burner) Peak The main peak of Fragrant Hill is 550 meters above sea level. Two giant rocks on top of it are named Breast Rocks. Standing on top of the rocks one has a grand view down bellow: a sea of clouds and trees.

重阳阁 为香炉峰顶的主体建筑,高10余米,是座观景楼。

Chongyang Tower The main structure on top of Xianglu Peak is 10 meters high, a good spot to review the scenery.

碧云寺　为西山名刹，建于 14 世纪中叶。全寺 6 层建筑依山顺势，次第排列，其中金刚宝座塔和五百罗汉堂最为著名。

Biyun (Azure Cloud) Temple Built in the mid-14th century, the six courtyards are arranged up a slope. The temple is famous for its 500 Arhat Hall and Diamond Throne.

五百罗汉　共 508 尊,各高 1.5 米,均为
木胎泥塑,外饰金箔;罗汉神态各异,是清代
雕塑艺术中的杰作。

500-Arhat Hall There are actually 508 statues of arhats in the hall, each 1.5 meters
high, made of clay but wrapped in gold
foil. They show the high sculpture skills
during the Qing Dynasty.

卧佛　供于香山卧佛寺,铜质,身长 5.2 米,重 25 吨,头西足东,面南而卧,像的东西北三面环立 12 尊彩色塑像。据传,这组佛像表现释迦牟尼临终时向 12 位弟子嘱咐后事的情景。

Sleeping Buddha The copper statue of Buddha in the Wuofo (Sleeping Buddha) Temple at the foot of Fragrant Hill is 5.2 meters long and weighs 25 tons. Around the Buddha on its eastern, western and northern sides stand 12 colored statues. Legend has it that this is the scene when Sakyamuni gave his last words to his 12 disciples on his deathbed.

阅武楼　　又名演武厅,是清代皇帝检阅八
旗官兵军事操练的城楼。

Yuewu (Reviewing the Army) Tower During the Qing Dynasty, the emperor often
came here to watch the army drilling.

编　　辑：望天星　　王　勇
翻　　译：刘宗仁
摄　　影：姜景余　　张肇基
　　　　　望天星　　高明义
　　　　　何炳富　　罗文发
　　　　　刘启俊　　黄韬朋
　　　　　严忠义　　魏铭祥
　　　　　牛嵩林　　董宗贵
　　　　　朱　钢　　胡维标
装帧设计：王　　志

Editors: Wang Tianxing and Wang Yong
Translated by: Liu Zongren
Photos by: Jiang Jingyu,　　Zhang Zhaoji,
　　　　　　　Wang Tianxing,　Gao Mingyi,
　　　　　　　He Bingfu,　　　Luo Wenfa,
　　　　　　　Liu Qijun,　　　Huang Taopeng,
　　　　　　　Yan Zhongyi,　　Wei Mingxiang,
　　　　　　　Niu Songlin,　　Dong Zonggui,
　　　　　　　Zhu Gang and Hu Weibiao
Designed by: Wang Zhi

北京名胜

望天星　王　勇　编

刘宗仁　　　　译

*

中国世界语出版社出版

北京 1201 工厂印制

中国国际图书贸易总公司发行(国际书店)

(中国北京车公庄西路 35 号)

邮政信箱第 399 号　邮政编码 100044

2000 年 2 月（16 开）第一版第五次印刷

ISBN 7－5052－0157－3/K·25(外)

06000

85－CE－422P